FREEDOM

Also by Sonny Barger

Dead in 5 Heartbeats

Ridin' High, Livin' Free

Hell's Angel

WILLIAM MORROW
An Imprint of HarperCollins*Publishers*

DOM
Credos from the Road

Sonny
Barger

HarperCollins books may be purchased for educational, business, or sales promotional use. For information please write: Special Markets Department, HarperCollins Publishers, 10 East 53rd Street, New York, NY 10022.

FIRST EDITION

Designed by Joel Avirom and Jason Snyder

Printed on acid-free paper

Library of Congress Cataloging-in-Publication Data

Barger, Sonny.
    Freedom : credos from the road / Sonny Barger with Keith and Kent Zimmerman.—1st ed.
        p.   cm.
    ISBN 0-06-053256-4 (acid-free paper)
    1. Liberty.   2. Conduct of life.   3. Leadership.   4. Motorcycling.
    5. Barger, Sonny.   I. Zimmerman, Keith.   II. Zimmerman, Kent,
    1953–   III. Title.

HM1266.B37 2005
646.7'00973—dc22   2005041572

---

05   06   07   08   09   WBC/RRD   10   9   8   7   6   5   4   3   2   1

Freedom is not just another word.

—Sonny Barger

CONTENTS

CONTENTS

Introduction

Live your life the Sonny Barger way? I don't recommend it.

I'm frequently asked about my philosophy of life and my views on freedom in America. I'm not sure how this came to be, people asking me these questions, but it has been so frequent as of late that I decided to put my thoughts down on paper and write a book about it.

Let me begin by saying that I'm a lifelong fan of the American way of life, particularly the way of life and the rules that our founding fathers mapped out for us a couple of centuries ago. To me, these rules are where freedom really lies. America was born out of a revolution staged by smart and tough renegades and radicals. Guys like Thomas Jefferson, Thomas Paine, Benjamin Franklin, and Samuel Adams are the quintessential American rebels, troublemakers and innovators who stayed loyal to one another and true to one single vision: freedom. When I say rebels I mean it. Funny how the word *rebel* has taken on an entire new meaning today.

My way of life is an American way of life that requires a never-ending devotion to the "idea of" and the
"practice of" freedom. Being aware of yourself and looking after your brothers, sisters, and partners means staying vigilant and aware at all times. As much as I'm
looking out at the road ahead, I'm tempted to look over
my shoulder, back at the legacy I am leaving behind, a
legacy of brotherhood, loyalty, fun times, and hell-
raising. But I can't and don't look back. I always look
ahead, to the side, but never back.

Writing *Freedom* made me ask myself a lot of serious, soul-searching bottom-line questions, questions
you'll need to ask yourself in the process of reading this
book. Who am I really? What are my strongest beliefs?
What exactly do I stand for and represent? What's
worth living for? What's worth dying for? What is my individual definition of freedom?

Only daredevil, freedom-loving Americans would take a
two-wheel, motorized contraption like a motorcycle,
wrench it up, turn it into a street-burning road machine,
and let it symbolize their notion of freedom. And get
away with it. Be allowed to do it, is more to the point.
During the early twentieth century in Europe, the motorcycle was a practical, dependable mode of transportation.

After World War II and probably as a result of the war it-self, we turned the motorcycle into a screaming batter-ing ram from hell with flames painted on the side. My friends and I put everything we owned into our bikes then. Our bikes were us, and to us, they were and remain the very symbols of freedom.

Another offshoot or result of the war was the brotherhood, commonality, and regimentation that we learned as soldiers. Joining a band of brothers together, a group with one common interest or mission, whether as a company, a team, or a motorcycle club, requires not only a commitment to loyalty but an understanding of self-preservation as well. You might ask why I do it. It was my choice to form an organization, and after I did so, it was my obligation to maintain it. A group only works if there is an established set of rules that all in-volved pledge to and maintain. When you are a member of an organization, life isn't only about you. As part of a circle of people who depend on one another, you watch one another's back and remain loyal to the concept of brotherhood. You learn how leadership and loyalty are about wedding your personal beliefs into a common be-lief, losing the individuality of thought and joining to-gether with others. This bonding yields freedom, believe it or not. That is one of the principles I will be addressing in this book. So I begin with this question: Are you ready to give yourself up to be free?

While I can't claim to be an expert on life management, I can sure tell you a few stories about the pursuit of happiness, and I can say that after fifty years on the road, the two biggest constants in my life are freedom and brotherhood.

Writing this book put my constants of freedom and brotherhood into personal perspective. It also helped me to gather my core beliefs and philosophy and put them down on paper in a straightforward, no-bullshit manner. In communicating my thoughts, I tried not to preach or rant. I tried to keep my thoughts and credos simple and direct, as if we were having a conversation. *Freedom* wasn't written as a political manifesto, although it might be perceived that way. Rather, I set out to convey equal contempt for all political parties, law enforcement organizations, and any organization or institution that tries to control me by separating me from my individual freedom. In other words: living free as an individual.

I'm not exactly sure how best to define the term *freedom*. It'll come forth as you read the book. What I have written here are my thoughts that were born on the road, at rest, and during periods of incarceration. Freedom just might be the most direct book about my life

that I've written. I've already gotten a hell of a lot out of writing it. If you get something out of reading it, well, then I've accomplished something.

Before we get started, though, here is a very simple question: Do you take freedom for granted?

Lose it and you won't.

I never considered myself a political person; in fact, I am apolitical, if you want a classification. But by living in the United States of America and riding a Harley-Davidson motorcycle, you become classified as a political statement in the flesh, like it or not. You are branded as a modern-day outlaw, a ne'er-do-well, an agitator, and yet we bike riders are only doing what we are allowed to do because we live in America. Freedom is what we all seek, but it's what we do with that freedom that ultimately defines our character. In the end, a man's character cements his fate, good or bad.

I'm neither Republican nor Democrat, more of an outsider not even looking in. You could classify me a libertarian (small *l*), an independent (small *i*) without any party or a political agenda. As a felon, I have lost the right to vote, but I still have my opinions and beliefs. My values and affiliations come from a quilt of mixed influences I've picked up along the road, in clubhouses, and in jail. I've also spent years on the receiving end of America's wrath and power, and while I love America, I have a lot of fun tasting and testing my freedom.

Every person alive is unique. As human beings, we are social animals, we have to interact with one another. It's been that way since the Garden of Eden. Interacting does not mean controlling or that one holds sway over another. It means the way you treat me is the way I will treat you. As an individual, you have your own unique set of rules for how you conduct yourself, and when they coincide with the rules of others, then this is harmony and life can be lived. When someone's rules are different from yours, that can be okay, but when they try to impose their rules on you, a problem arises. Lots of problems arise. I don't think anyone likes to be told what they have to do.

Law and *order* are terms that are thrown around very loosely these days. As often as I've been branded a rebel, in my opinion I have a deeper belief in law and order than the average citizen, and I'm constantly repelled by the way overzealous authorities such as policemen or politicians don't share that view.

I'm one of those guys who, as the system tests me, continually challenges the system. I have seen our government trample on our most basic and hardest-won

freedoms and human rights, yet most Americans are too blind or comfortable to notice. People need a social system of their own. Inside that system they cooperate with others to achieve things that as individuals they could not achieve on their own. Law and order is an example of the principles that the democratic system has set up in order to achieve harmony.

The first motorcycle ride I took changed my life forever. So did serving a long-term sentence in Folsom. They were both equally important and monumental turning points in my life.

I'll begin with my initial motorcycle ride, which let me experience total freedom for the first time. When I was thirteen I had a little motor scooter that cost about twenty bucks. But I could get that little thing up to about forty miles an hour. A few years later, when I got out of the army, I graduated up to a full-size motorcycle. I had dabbled with cars, but I liked motorcycles because they were all you and nothing else. You could take the motor out and rev it up and then when you hit either the streets or highway, it was your creation and the world was yours. You could go as fast and as far as you wanted. It was freedom all right.

The second thing that has changed my life is that

I've done time in a few joints and county jails. In a lot of ways, I find jail, and especially prison, an all-American experience. No other country in the world puts more of its citizens in jail than America does. We lock up over two million people in this country at any given time. The prisoners range from out-and-out bad guys like cold-blooded murderers, child molesters, and big-time thieves to teenagers busted for their first offense dealing in drugs or prostitution. But no matter what you are in for, once you're in, you're in. In the joint everybody's the same, they're prisoners.

Prison is a place where the inmates, wardens, correctional officers, and whoever else is running the show fashions their own society, their own system. Both the people who run the prisons and the inmates who live there create their own little America, except it's an "America" with a much more intense set of rules, values, pecking order, privileges, routine, and punishments. In order to survive in this prison system, you have to be superaware and smart. You have to be self-confident and, above all, constantly on top of your immediate surroundings. You need to be capable of sizing up a bunch of different situations quickly. You have to be a swift judge of character and committed to the principle of getting through life one day at a time. As a result of this system, prison gave me an invaluable perspective on freedom and survival.

Prison, to me, was a job. I was working for a company, an organization meticulously built upon a foundation of strict rules and routines, with many decisions already made for you. You wake up when you're told to. Report to work detail. Eat your meals when you're told to. Go "home." Lights-out. There're the occasional lockdown, setback, good days, bad days, and horrible days. You lose control over your daily life. In such a situation, you're more conscious of the precious few moments that are your own. And those few moments for a prisoner are your freedom. And that is how I learned the true definition of "freedom."

Prison keeps people apart by relegating them to small and manageable subgroups guaranteed to keep them separate, hostile, slightly jealous of one another, and competing. Sound familiar? We end up doing "the man's" dirty work much more effectively than the man could do. In prison, after you're given a number, cell, and bunk, you're inside a social structure that's designed to erase your individuality out of you. It's a dehumanizing technique to the maximum, and without exception, it works beautifully. You can fight it but you'll eventually learn you won't win trying to do it your way. Do your job, do what is expected of you, and you win.

Look around at your own circumstances right now, your job, home, and organization. Do stubbornness and barriers divide you or do a common mission, interests, and goals unite you? You know the answer. When was the last time your family, fellow employees, or friends sat down and really discussed what keeps your group together? Is there a common goal that everyone understands, shares, and aspires to realize?

Before going into prison, I was accustomed to all the amenities that freedom in America brought. So I assumed that my freedom was a highly portable state of mind. But then, there I was in Folsom Prison, with only a few basic rights afforded to me. I soon learned that bringing that "portable" sense of freedom into a prison cell while serving a potential life sentence was a far different challenge. Since my body was confined, I learned to free my mind. It was this self-ownership of mind and thus spirit that got me through.

But this liberation of mind and spirit did not come to me overnight. While I was inside, I received boxes of books from the outside. These were the "Free Sonny Barger" days of 1973 and 1974, when my then wife, Sharon, and my friends worked tirelessly to keep my name out in front of the press.

I am a self-taught individual. My schooling stopped early and I was never inspired by my parents and surroundings when I was young enough to read a book, or read anything for that matter. I could read but I never appreciated or knew how much reading can do for you until I was in Folsom. The books I got there were of all different types. There were novels that, I learned, give you a chance to escape to different worlds, experience and meet people from all walks of life, see situations that otherwise you would never have known existed. There were nonfiction books that I learned from, books of history and politics, and also biographies. A whole new world opened up to me and slowly I began to realize that everything that mattered really was determined by the state of mind I was in. I could be doing some menial job during the day, but if my mind was off somewhere else, then I was starting to achieve an inner freedom.

Today, I know almost as much about doing jail time and loss of freedom as I do about riding motorcycles and enjoying liberty and bliss. From the 1950s on up to the present, I served about thirteen lucky years. As I got more proficient at doing time behind bars, I also began envisioning freedom in the form of a collection of credos, which is what I'm now passing on to you in this book. These are my "pearls," taken originally from notes, letters, and notebooks, now assembled into a book of thoughts and advice.

After finishing my last five-year prison stretch at a federal facility in Phoenix in 1992, I decided to leave Oakland permanently. I settled in Arizona, only a couple miles away from where I'd once been confined. Once I was established, there I was again, a free American, beginning anew, free to ride, write, and raise my own hell. In short, I was able to exercise my freedom.

The greatest thing that I have learned is probably the simplest thing any of us can learn: I am what I am. I've opted for the rough road in life, the one less traveled. And I think I've got a few things to reveal. My life has been a good one, but one full of setbacks, hard times, and disappointments, punctuated by achievements, good times, hard-fought battles, and significant victories. So having lived in both restricted and unrestricted conditions, I feel I have definite and unique opinions on the subject of freedom. I've lived with both an overabundance and a complete shortage of it. And ironically, it was during my complete shortage period that I learned the most about the concept of freedom.

My most basic credo is: I never said freedom was cheap. And it ain't. Never will be. It's been the highest-priced and most precious commodity of my life. Johnny

Cash used to say the best part of a journey is the last mile home. I've found independence to be a hell of a ride, a hard ride, never a dull ride, guaranteed to be a bumpy ride, always unpredictable, but well worth the long trip home, especially that last mile, which I am riding into free.

1 Treat Me Good, I'll Treat You Better. Treat Me Bad, I'll Treat You Worse.

Be careful how you treat people. It can come back either to help you or come back and bite you on the ass.

Nobody ever confused me with being a priest, a minister, or a holy man. "Treat me good, I'll treat you better; treat me bad I'll treat you worse" is my personal take on "Do unto others as you would have others do unto you." Except with a modern edge. The phrase is on a plaque and is hung on an honored spot on my wall, whether at my cycle shops, my office, at home, or in the garage. It serves as a warning to whoever reads it. I'm a serious, determined man destined to be treated fairly.

I like to take fairness to its logical extreme. When somebody bucks the trend by really going out of his or her way, by going the extra mile and respecting me as opposed to treating me rudely or behaving like an asshole or an idiot, I respond by treating him or her better. People are like animals, and I mean that in a good way. Horses. Dogs. Cats. I love animals because they instinctively respond to kindness and discipline with loyalty. Kindness, like violence, can be an effective tool, especially when it's unexpected. When somebody is fair and decent, everybody wins, everybody's happy. But if somebody dares burn me, look out. Rip me off or steal my bike and you'll be nursing broken bones and drinking salt water.

On an everyday level, there's the example of the guy at the bar pushing you out of the way and stepping on your toes in order to get himself a beer. Three things to consider in this situation: he's either trying to prove something to you, he's showing off to his compadres, or he is in desperate need of a drink and is oblivious to his actions and the world around him.

Let's start by discussing the third. He's got his own troubles and not worth bothering with. The first guy is something you have to obviously deal with and right away. The second guy, these are the unpredictables and they'll do about anything to show that they are something they aren't, namely tough.

Guys, especially those just out of prison, notice immediately how rude our society has become. Inside the joint, it's "excuse me" and "pardon me, brother." Outside, it's "outta the way, buddy." Dog-eat-dog way of life. Think about it: What is it like where you live and work, and how do you deal with it?

Another example of being treated badly that annoys the hell out of me is not communicating. If someone tells me they'll get back to me or give me an answer to something and they simply don't get back, it says to me they don't give a shit either about the situation or me or both. It's not being treated fairly, and when the situation arises when they ask you for something, your natural tendency then is to not deal with it at all. If you don't respond, then you're playing the game, too. Treat someone the way you want to be treated.

It reminds me of a story a fellow bike rider told me about being in the navy. When he was assigned duty on a ship, he and all of its crew sailed out into the Pacific Ocean to begin a series of military maneuvers. The first couple of days out, he kept hearing the words *Roger Wilco* and he started wondering who this guy Roger Wilco was that everyone was talking about. So he asked some other sailor and he laughed and told him it was part of the basic etiquette in the navy and stood for "Roger," "will comply." First used in the signaling system, it later came to be used when orders were given by a superior and the inferior would make the gesture of saying "Wilco," to signify not only that he had heard him but that the order would be done. That to me is respect and compliance.

When somebody treats you good, see to it that you

respond to them. It can be with a simple thank-you and/or a nod. Then you come across as the noble one, as appreciative, a rare quality in an individual these days. And guess what—what you give is what you get. People value respect; they fight against the opposite. Treat someone badly and it is bound to come back at you sometime. And it does, just when you don't expect it.

There was a young man that joined the club and I immediately noticed that he was being a bit reclusive and standoffish. I liked him and had definitely voted for him to be inducted; I just felt that maybe he wasn't feeling too comfortable yet, was a bit intimidated, and had a little fear. I approached him and told him first that I was glad he was with us, then asked him to clean up some of the trash and garbage that had gathered behind the headquarters. That's all it took. He respected me for approaching him one-on-one and he respected the fact that I told him to do something as well. He became a brother for life and one of the best members an organization could ever have. Very dependable.

2 Put Together Your Own Family

Can you rely on your family? What if you could choose the members of your family?

My mother abandoned my sister, my father, and me. My father drank himself to death. My older sister and I learned to fend for ourselves. I'm not remorseful or crying about my life; I have happy memories of my childhood. All that talk about parents holding you back doesn't wash with me. Blaming your mother is just another way of clinging to her. While I've had the benefit of living and growing up in simpler times, I did not fully understand the meaning and feeling of family until I formed my own.

When I'm asked about family, my reply is simple. Five words.

My friends are my family.

My definition of family is someone who will do anything for you, anytime, anywhere, without regard for their own health and safety. I don't need much of a reason to help out a member of "my family." It's a natural reflex. One of the things the cops keep forgetting about motorcycle riders is that we tend to stick together. And even if you have never climbed onto a motorcycle in your life, you should remember this, too.

I remember a judge looking down on us from his high bench, getting ready for a hot and heavy conspiracy trial. All through the pretrial bail hearings, the cops were boasting about how bad I was, that I was a flight risk. Then, peering through his spectacles, after it came up that one of our friends had put his farm on the line so that another friend could make bail, the judge looked astonished. He asked, "You'd honestly put your house and home on the line for somebody who's not even related?" He was stunned. "I wouldn't."

To which the friend replied, "That's where we differ, Your Honor. We do."

The judge was impressed and immediately granted bail.

Of course the friend that put his farm up got his money back. I didn't skip bail and went through the trial as I had planned to.

Part of the beauty of my "family" is the unquestioning, steadfast support we give to one another. If I'm sitting in jail, I don't have to sit and worry about making bail or getting out. I know that my "family" on the outside is on the case, trying to work things out. I also know that my girlfriend has someone looking out for her. For most inmates, the safety of their family might be a primary concern. For me, my family is not even a remote worry. I can concentrate on other things, like a defense.

You might be thinking, having such a "support group" is a privilege only extended to someone like me, a fifty-plus-year rider. I'm here to say that my family extends the same treatment—from the oldest to the youngest of our people. Everybody helps the others in times of trouble.

I'm not here to lecture you on the breakdown of the American familial, social, or corporate system, although I find it deplorable that even blood brothers and sisters fail to look after one another. That's partly the reason we have so many homeless people living on the streets today. There seems to be a lack of commitment to extended family. I remain committed to my core family as one I can trust and depend on. The end result is the assurance that I'm surrounded by the people who will help me, stick by me, and fight alongside me, through good and bad, life and death.

It all comes by selecting the right people for your own "family," loving them, abiding by them, respecting them, and treating them as equals on all levels, an extended household of commonality.

3 Stick Together, Even If It Means Taking One for the Team

Stick together and people will think twice before messing with you.

When I was standing trial on RICO charges, I reaped the benefits of victory by simply locking arms with my brothers. By sticking together, we created an unprecedented and united front against those who attacked or opposed us. Along the way, quite a few loyal friends took one for the team. Like the song says, "All gave some, some gave all."

RICO—Racketeer Influenced and Corrupt Organizations—is a federal law originally designed to prosecute criminal groups. With RICO firmly in place, the feds first came after the mobsters. After they had been divided and suppressed, next came the motorcycle clubs. Now RICO targets all organizations, from companies, street gangs, terrorist organizations, labor unions, protesters, religious groups, bookstore owners, bankers, Wall Street investment firms, doctors, cops, and politicians, whatever. Through the group's association with one member who has done something illegal, they try to bring down the whole group. (RICO is a good example of a law whose original bad intentions have run further amok.)

A lot of organizations crumbled under the pressures of RICO prosecution. When the long arm of the law tapped you on the shoulder—or more accurately, kicked your door down and charged you with RICO—it was time to fold up the tents, rat out your friends, and plead guilty. It was the convenient way of getting a lesser sentence. "It wasn't me . . . it was all of us!"

But not me. I didn't take that road. I was the first to lock arms and make a rule. Nobody pleads out. Some might do time, but nobody points the finger at another friend. Nobody testifies against another part of the team. We stick together, even if it means hard sacrifice.

I once was being held at the Manhattan Correctional Center for not cooperating with a grand-jury investigation in New York. While there, I met a couple of mobsters. They were curious about how I had been able to be found innocent. I told them just what I'm telling you. We did it by staying focused, and most of all, by not turning on one another and maintaining a united front. It's much easier for an antagonistic force to push around one individual than mess with a team of fifty, who are all standing tall, and ready and willing to fight as one.

I was the first individual to successfully defend against RICO. Later on, friends went on to beat conspiracy charges, notably in Kentucky, using the same strategy. After a long and costly trial in Kentucky, even the judge recognized the fact that we had stayed unified as one force. We had not changed what we had initially said at the beginning of the trial. This unwavering quality is what the judge respected.

As a result, I took the heat and served almost five years while my other friends were acquitted. (The only other friend convicted besides me died fighting outside a bar a few days before having to serve his sentence in a federal penitentiary in Atlanta.) Everyone else was set free.

Serving almost five years in the pen might not sound like a victory to you, but it was to me. I believe my conviction helped keep a couple dozen of my friends out of the pen. That's when I began writing. I left the federal prison stronger, smarter, and more respected.

The lesson is this: Betrayal and blame in the long run won't get you what you want. If you are guilty, you pay the price. Pulling others in to try to save your own ass does not work. Work with your group if you have one. Numbers rule.

4 Recognize Your Enemies!

Everyone is not on the same side. I can attest to that.

I've had plenty of disagreements in my life and they've stemmed mostly from people out to get me for what I had done to them or represented to them. The lines of demarcation are pretty hard to see at times and you have to turn your radar on. Keep it on. It's constant vigilance.

With the authorities and the cops it's easy. You assume they're thinking, *I'm right, you're wrong.* I play by the rules and I know it, so they got nothing on me.

It's the other, more subtle enemies that you have to watch out for.

While I was touring for my first book, I got a lot of calls from the national press for interviews and appearances, from the newspapers and magazines, radio and television. I felt it was a duty to myself and to the publisher to do as many as I could and get as much exposure as I could. I did a lot of them, but I skipped some, too.

The ones I skipped were ones where I felt like I was getting set up, that there was an agenda and they wanted me to perform for them or say something that they wanted to hear. Something they could sell. Media is a business, after all.

When I was asked to appear on the program *Politically Incorrect,* it seemed like a perfectly reasonable thing to do. Not that I am a political person in any sense of the word, but it was a program that a lot of people were watching at the time. When they asked me to report to the studios at a certain time, I was there early. But I sensed something funny was going on. I was told shortly after getting there that there was to be no rehearsal. I wasn't given any type of script and I wasn't even introduced to the host.

Suddenly I was put on a stage and a producer who was off behind a camera started counting down: "Twenty-five seconds . . . twenty seconds . . . fifteen seconds . . . "—this being the amount of time before the cameras would start rolling and I would be on live television. I thought, *Fuck this,* and got up, walked across the stage and out of the studio, got on my bike, and rode away.

Later I learned that the *Politically Incorrect* team did have a whole set of questions for me and one of them had to do with getting me to talk about all the sex-slave girls in motorcycle clubs. Yeah, right.

The lesson here is, keep those you don't know or trust either at a distance or out of your life altogether. It's that simple. The "others" are the enemy until they prove they are not. I've lived by this rule so far in my life and it has worked. Trust yourself first and the others second, but recognize the enemy at all times.

5 Leaders Exhibit Strength, While Bullies Prey on Weakness

I can't stand bullies. No one really can, but few go up against them. Many times bullies can turn into rats and liars. Bullies use their physical (and sometimes mental) strength to gain control of a situation.

When I spot a bully, I act immediately, decisively, and sometimes violently. Then I step back and try to look deeper. What's motivating this guy? Why does he do what he does? That's where I find problems. People show their true colors when they become loose and comfortable around a group of like-minded individuals. So pay close attention to any warning signs before you accept someone inside your organization. "All talk and no walk" is a problem. Boastful behavior. Preying on smaller people or workers further down the chain of command. Cocky behavior. Think of yourself honestly and be honest and objective. Despite the strengths this person might possess, don't ignore their weaknesses and liabilities, and trust your instincts. Give yourself ample time to check out and get to know any potential new team members you're ready to take on.

Bullies I've known in the past usually had a father or a big brother or an elder who drank or slapped them around as boys. Later in life, a bully puts on a facade, a bluff and show of superiority. It's what worked on them when they were younger. Outside, they're big and tough. Inside, they feel weak, rejected, and vulnerable. Bullying others gives them a temporary high. Once that high fades, they go back to their pathetic natures and the cycle begins over again. Bullying is a prime example of weakness hiding as strength.

In the end, a bully can endanger your entire organization by chasing the most valuable people away and by taking a lot of good people down with them. A bully can be a convincing sort and hard to spot a lot of the time. They are people out to hurt, frighten, or tyrannize those they feel are below them. The original bullies were thugs hired by the rich in order to get things done. Because they worked for the rich, they felt they were superior.

Today, a bully can be a coworker who screams in the office just to get things done his way, or it could be a cop who uses his shield to hide behind and push people around. Whenever or wherever you find them, don't trust them and don't give them the time of day.

Having a bully in your organization in the end makes you vulnerable. As a member of the group, you have to do something. Don't be afraid to confront them because bullies crumble at any sign of strength. I've seen examples of bullies ratting out their own people, selling themselves out to the competition in exchange for flattery and approval. The last thing you need during any type of confrontation is that kind of disloyalty and weakness.

A bully in your midst, pushing people around, is a major warning signal, and whoever's running the show in your organization has the obligation and responsibility to step in and quickly take care of the situation. Otherwise, the rank and file will take matters into their own hands, and as a leader, you don't want that.

Bullies bring nothing to the table except themselves and their own needs and wants. They lack loyalty and they are not the warriors they pretend to be. Weed them out of the group, and put them out with the trash, where they belong.

6 Screw Fightin' Fair

Do you fight fair or do you fight to win?

People sometimes rap me for my practice of rat-packing. In other words, when you pick on one of my friends, you'll immediately have to contend with all of us. The situation turns ugly in a hurry. People get hurt. Now let me ask you a question. When your friend or loved one is fighting—winning or losing—do you idly stand by and watch them defend themselves? I hope your answer is no.

Neither do I.

I've learned to live with the fact that the first things tossed out of the ring in the heat of combat are benevolence and mercy. When you're fighting for your life, your pride, or your dignity, all rules based on courtesy are suspended. There is only one objective at this point and that is to win the fight by any means necessary.

You have to enter a fight with two things: the knowledge of what you are fighting for and winning as your only objective. Once you have your conviction straight (and lots of times this will have to be a decision made in a split second), act on it and quickly. The first punch is usually the one that gets the attention of your opponent and makes the difference.

A few years ago, at a book signing and swap meet, a group decided to invade our gathering with weapons, clubs, knives, and baseball bats. The first of our crew at the scene was severely outnumbered. He had his conviction straight and he went for it, initiated the battle, and didn't hem and haw around waiting for backup, which, of course, came quickly. I was proud when I heard what he had done. He charged into the situation with a "take no prisoners" attitude. But it wasn't too long before an entire group jumped in to help. By the time I arrived, the situation was well under control. The invasion was contained within minutes, even before the cops came to "restore order." It was a concentrated effort by a team that put a lid on any further violence that day. That didn't stop the cops from arresting some friends. Months later, my friends were completely exonerated and acquitted.

In times of trouble, if one of your friends is in difficulty, jump in and help. You won't see me standing by in a bar, watching one of my friends in a fight, slugging it out alone. Screw fighting fair. The health and safety of my cause and comrades far outweigh what others might think of me. If the odds and numbers happen to tip in your favor, then so be it. If not, kick ass anyway the best you can. Then, later, call in all your friends and make your adversaries pay dearly.

7 An Organization Can't Be All Chiefs and No Indians

To become a leader, first you've got to join the group. Sounds simple but it is not.

Let's take the example of a couple of guys in a bar. One scribbles an idea on a napkin. The other guy looks at it and agrees. They vow to ride together and watch each other's back out on the street. These two individuals become one and inseparable and thus a small organization of sorts is born.

In my particular case, the organization I joined was a motorcycle club. It was a group of disenfranchised people who thought that they were the only ones on the planet who felt unfulfilled, unsatisfied, on the outside, and out of step with the mainstream. That's not a bad thing. These are the type of people, the renegades and the castoffs tired of going it alone, who might be your first "joiners." From there, as your organization evolves, leaders will begin to emerge from within.

There is one type who inspires others to walk a little taller and straighter, the one individual who can listen and talk to everyone, who acts for himself when he acts for the group. And then there are those who are good at taking direction. It is not that these are "weaker" individuals or that they lack stamina; they are soldiers who trust and respect the group as a whole and are able to take direction from a leader they trust and respect. The leader guides the group.

Are you considering becoming a leader? Have you worked with an organization long enough to know how it really works?

When the first club I was in got off the ground, I was kind of coached by another biker member who had a mind for organization. We talked about things like membership dues, meetings, rules, and what struck me most was that everything he was describing was a lot like the U.S. Army.

The army is structured on a ranking system and you work your way up the ranks based on merit and performance and the exhibition of leadership qualities. You don't become a sergeant without having been a private. As a sergeant, you have more responsibility than a private, but you also have to report to someone above you as well, who in turn reports to . . . thus the chain of command.

This system seemed in the past to work very well

and indeed it did. So well that it still works today. I used a lot of the protocol I saw and learned from the U.S. Army in assembling my first club.

Work on it, think about it, and try to realize your own leadership potential, and don't forget to encourage someone else's as well. Not that everyone even aspires to be a leader, and that is natural. Some people are just born followers.

Trust Is Not a Weakness

Do you have someone close to you who will lay it all down for you without batting an eye? I do.

I can always depend on my best friend. He's my homey, the perfect cell mate, my soul brother, my missing piece, the other half. Out on the street, rain or shine, night or day, he's there and game for anything. Even when a motorcycle ride from Oakland to San Jose was like a cross-country trip, he was there. In a heartbeat he was always ready to ride. It is the trust between us that keeps us bonded. I don't feel any less of a person or weaker when I turn to him for advice, help, or just someone to listen. We understand each other and have for a long time.

When I moved from Oakland to Arizona, that same friend packed his gear as well. After more than forty years of riding the Oakland streets together, we migrated to the great Southwest, surprising everyone who couldn't begin to imagine us ever leaving Oakland and

making such a radical change. But we did it, and my friend now lives about fifty miles down the road from me, the Arizona equivalent of a neighbor.

You can't have too many close friends. Luckily, I've cultivated quite a few of them throughout my life. Through my relationships with my friends, I've learned how to trust. Especially on the road, having a good friend riding close by is the equivalent of having an extra set of senses. He helps prevent me from being careless and stupid. I ride at my best with my friends around.

In prison, you can't put a price tag on a friendship or on trust, having someone watching your back. Most people are able to honestly count on one hand the number of people they would trust with their lives. For me, that list could go into the dozens, a long list of people I've learned from and people who have learned from me. People who keep their friends and comrades at arm's length often find the world a very cold and lonely place.

Whatever the bond that binds you (for me, it's motorcycles), a strong mutual interest with a core of best friends you trust will help you live a longer and straighter life. These comrades are the guys who will pull you back when you cross over the line, who will pick you up when you fall over the edge, who will make sure you don't have to go it alone. We don't ride alone.

I guess the strongest example of trust or brotherhood today is a motorcycle club. We did what we wanted to do, together. We knew the virtues of an organization that was based on depending on one another and none of us was any weaker for it. No one ever thought less of us for it, either.

9 Stay Alert in the Pack. What Happens to You Happens to the Rider Behind You.

Be vigilant and aware. Those living and working next to you are depending on it.

Riding in a forty-bike pack is the ultimate exercise in teamwork and the most definitive example of harmony I know. Consider it the domino effect on wheels; one small screwup in the fast lane can result in the catastrophic downfall of the entire group. If you're part of a well-oiled outfit traveling ninety miles per hour in close wheel-to-wheel formation, there's no wiggle room in the execution. Not only must you trust those who are immediately in front of and behind you, but each and every rider up and down the line, from the pack leader to those bringing up the rear, are all interconnected by riding and working in close proximity. Riding like this is a rush that gives everyone involved equal power and authority over one another's fate.

It takes know-how and courage. The ride does not require an explanation, just participants.

It is also an exercise of trust and character within a situation of life and death. Every rock, pothole, or tire scrap you meet on the road affects the guy behind you, and so on down the line. Since everyone's reflexes are equally vital, no matter how much partying you've done the night before, when you assume your position in the pack, your senses and talent for anticipating the actions of those behind you and in front of you must be second to none. Just being on top of your game isn't enough. You've got to crawl inside the hearts, minds, and souls of everybody else riding in the pack. On the highway, at ninety-plus miles per, there's no such thing as one rider who's more important than another. The pack needs to be a well-timed centipede, a mighty machine, every moving part equal, vital, and well oiled.

Cruising along a straight highway with good weather and no traffic isn't too much of a challenge. It requires that all riders keep an even distance apart. But anytime there is a curve, each rider needs to adjust his speed and carefully track the path of those ahead, not to rear-end them or veer into the rider beside him. The pack, as determined by its leader, may also have to snake around traffic or other road obstacles in order to stay together as one group, or divide temporarily until the interruption is passed. Add the complications that come from the elements like wind, fog, or rain, and the riding gets even more hazardous and challenging. Maybe someone's bike has a malfunction, runs out of gas, or leaks oil. The bigger the pack and the faster it goes, the more likely some tiny factor will be amplified to cause potential disaster. Managing all these variables successfully is a daunting task in which only the fittest survive.

The pack-riding experience is an extreme experience. Life in the fast lane, as they say. At its best, you are moving as gracefully and majestically as the wind. At its worst, you're scattered across the highway. In seconds you can go from an impressive formation of riders to a pile of bleeding flesh, broken bones, broken glass, spilled fuel, burned rubber, and twisted steel.

I seriously doubt you'll find a better example of a team of people living, breathing, moving, and reacting in sync as a group. A lot has been said and written about a group acting as one. Here's my ultimate illustration. You have to become one with your partners. No choice. Together you enter a state of elevated achievement only through mutual skill, practice, and trust.

A successful ride happens when we anticipate one another's moves, even limitations. As a pack, we regularly put our lives and fates into one another's hands. It's only through working as a seamless unit that we reach our final destination or goals, ride after ride after ride.

Stay alert by keeping your eyes and all other senses not only on the road ahead of you, but also on the rider in front of you and behind you. By looking out for your partners, you're also looking out for yourself.

10) Tradition Just Gets Your Engine Started. You Drive the Bike.

As a member of the next generation, what are you bringing to the table to keep your organization going and up-to-date?

Try to remember the reason you started riding a motorcycle in the first place. For me, it was a couple of things but mostly rebellion. It was partly the movie *The Wild One* with Lee Marvin. There was also the initial rush of getting up on two wheels and riding against the wind. There was also the power and the rumble of the bike and the look on the faces of the girls as you drove up on your Harley. There was the look on the faces of their boyfriends as their girlfriends looked at you riding on your bike. On a bike, suddenly you had a 360-degree view of the countryside (before helmets were mandatory) and you were roaring down the interstate. But mainly you rode for a reason—to be different, right? And to be able to hang out with a core of buddies who actually rode, and who weren't afraid to shake things up, to fight, raise hell, get laid, get high, and ride fast.

My point is that we did this for a reason. We weren't just blindly following tradition. Invent your own styles and systems. Don't be enslaved and trapped by the past and a particular look. Shake up the institution you're a part of. Change things. Move the furniture around. Change the lightbulbs. Stand up to the older generation who prefer it their way and are intimidated by the challenge of creating a new subset and a newer mind-set. It is the same process that me and my young friends created by inventing a new look for riding our own customized Harleys. We did that literally by reinventing the Harley-Davidson from the ground up and by conforming to our own vision and not that of the motorcycle company and the dealers. We converted our machines from what we considered to be loaded-down garbage wagons to sleek, stylish choppers. We also transformed the old-fashioned concept of Sunday-afternoon motorcycling into a key ingredient of the new counterculture of sex, drugs, and rock and roll. We became labeled as the one-percenters that gave motorcyclists a bad reputation. In turn, we gave an established, staid, and stodgy organization like Harley-Davidson a new lease on life. They started selling a lot more bikes to a younger demographic.

Create your own new one percent. Just as we found

a new way of horrifying the establishment of weekend riders, young riders of today are rebelling in their way by showing a preference for speed. They favor faster and modern brands of European or Japanese sport bikes to Harleys. These are the bikes that are now leaving Harleys in the dust, and are bikes that, out of the box, can get up to speeds of over a hundred to a hundred and twenty miles per hour in a matter of seconds.

Go beyond the bikes and bike clubs for a second. Think about becoming the individual that you want to be and not something your peers or parents expect you to be. Do it your way and don't keep looking for constant approval. It will come in time if you are true to your own instincts and passions. Be true to yourself, everything else will follow.

A word of warning. When you break new earth, you'll instantly be considered an outsider. You're bound to meet lots of resistance from the old guard. When you create something new and unique, it's harder for the old guys to dismiss and judge you by the same old (un)reliable standards.

Without an infusion of new ideology, institutions are doomed to become just that—institutions. They become parodies and clichéd versions of themselves, or worse, complacent and established relics and rituals of the past. They hang on to tradition and hide behind it.

Whatever you do to distinguish yourself will necessarily involve some kind of danger, some kind of risk, and the challenge of doing something new. No risk, no gain. It's up to you to keep it interesting and new and, most important, you.

11 Leaders Accept Dissent, the Tyrant Goes It Alone

Can you handle an honest disagreement?

Many leaders like to think that they surround themselves with the brightest, the toughest, and the best, but how many have the balls to surround themselves with the most honest?

As Americans with less than three hundred years of heritage, we rose from the spirit of violence, rebellion, and revolution to become a nation of doubters and dissenters. It's in our genes to stand up and disagree. That's the cloth Americans are cut from. Thomas Jefferson did not firmly believe in democracy, but he sure as hell felt strongly about liberty. And in many people's heads, there was no stronger defender of the American way than Thomas Jefferson.

There's bound to be lots of disagreement and dissent among defiant individuals. When you surround yourself with dyed-in-the-wool individualists, that's the cost.

The organization that I belonged to was filled with individualists, tall, short, smart, not so smart, funny, morose, etc., but we were a group and had one thing in common: we all liked to ride motorcycles and that was the common denominator. When there was dissension (and you can surely believe there was), we always got back to the common good of all, and as the leader, I had the job of making that decision.

Tyrants are always right because they insist they are. They don't listen to anyone but themselves anyway. Leaders listen and act accordingly.

As a leader, don't confuse honest dissent with disloyalty or subversion. Take dissent and criticism as it's intended (provided it's honest). Listen hard. And don't take it personally. Good dissent may come from that lone, brave friend and colleague who will save you from making the biggest mistake or the worst decision of your life.

12 If You Want to Travel Fast, Travel Light

Strip away the excess baggage inside your brain and move through your problems and obstacles faster. You weren't born on drugs, with a two-pack-a-day cigarette habit or a drinking problem. Why not streamline yourself and clean up. If you're using, take a week off from the substances. Can you do it? You can if you want to.

When I originally stripped my bike down, it was to lighten the load and reduce wind resistance. It was a bumpy, rigid ride, but when you're young, the rough ride only makes you tougher and able to face a lot of things, because nothing is easy. But it was the simplicity of the stripped-down bike that I dug. I didn't really need or want all those mirrors and saddlebags and aerials and fancy partner seats. I wanted to ride by myself—fast and my way.

Too many people complicate their lives by trying to have it all: the career, the money, the family, the respect, too many friends, too many cars, and too many bed-

rooms in an empty house. It's like the bike with so many gadgets on it that you forget why you're even riding it.

Why? The material things become the only things that matter. People lose themselves. They forget about what true friendship and loyalty are and what it means to have things that you cannot touch. They lose their way, the road has far too many forks, and they forget where they are going. They complicate their lives by keeping everything in their head and don't face a problem and take care of it. They avoid problems and hope they will go away.

They don't take the time to strip down their bikes, create a plan, and move down the highway.

13 Temper the Steel to Forge a Strong Blade

Bad times set you back. Hard times can make you tougher.

Some say good soldiers are born not made. I don't fully agree. True, some warriors are born healthy and strong. Others need to be strengthened under extreme heat and pressure, like a diamond from a lump of coal, like a forged blade.

Life is one long boot camp, and only extreme and strenuous life experience can turn you into the complete soldier. When the bad times come along, don't complain. They're part of life.

What can you do?

Educate yourself and go to school. If not right now, soon. I dropped out of high school because I thought I knew all that I needed to know. Yet it wasn't until Folsom Prison that it dawned on me that an education would benefit me in the long run. I might have initially done it to prove to myself that I could start my "reeducation" program from scratch. I literally entered a program on the elementary-school level and quickly worked my way up the educational ladder. I obtained an AA degree in a few short years. Education is often wasted on the young in the sense that they see no practical application for it, since they haven't really lived life yet. For adults, the combination of life experiences with education is a perfect fit and makes perfect sense.

Think about joining some branch of the service, like the army. What I learned in the service helped me immeasurably. I was introduced to the concepts of loyalty, order, and chain of command. I came to understand that not only knowledge but also discipline was valuable. I developed a strong sense of brotherhood. I hardened my body and mind while developing a keen sense of survival. Once there were other people depending on me, I took life more seriously. I also had a great time meeting and hanging out with guys I probably never would have met or even approached on the street. I got along with different kinds of people from all different parts of the country. I got a strong, immediate sense of how big and diverse America was. The army worked for me. I made it work for me.

If you get thrown in jail, learn from it. I garnered as much knowledge about life in jail as I did in any school and the army combined. Jail slows down time. You need

to speed it back up. Reading occupies the hours and allows you to learn something. Your jail job can help fill up the days. Classes educate you and turn the days into weeks. Court appeals can break up the months. Jail teaches you a different type of survival game than the army. The army prepares you for the jungle overseas. Jail prepares you for the jungle on the streets. Confinement teaches you to be resourceful and grateful for the small things in life, from a family visit to a simple piece of fruit.

In short, what doesn't kill you makes you stronger. If jail and prison don't break you, they will make you stronger. Prison made me stronger, and I left with an education, the will to write an autobiography, and a buff body.

School. Army. Jail. These are a few basic life experiences that prepared me for the hard times and the long ride ahead. They are the life experiences that tempered me, and allowed me to find strength and direction in adversity. After tempering myself, I was ready for anything "the man" or whoever had to throw at me, and believe me, I've had the whole combination plate including the enchiladas thrown at me over the years.

14 Early Is On Time, On Time Is Late

Vince Lombardi time is ten minutes early.

One of the hardest things to get accustomed to once I got released from prison was people who were late. Life in jail is run on a strict routine. If you're not on the right side of the cell door when it's being racked, you're screwed. You're punished for losing track of the time.

A world where it's standard procedure to be "fashionably late" was a concept I had trouble getting used to.

If you deal with me (or anybody you respect), be on time. I'll go as far as to say, if you can't be early, don't even bother showing. Keeping me waiting tells me all I need to know about you. You don't consider my time, or yours, valuable. Worse, you're judging my concept of time by yours, which disregards and disrespects the sanctity I may feel for time. I've "done time" when time was an endless stretch in front of me. And I've experienced the reverse. After I was diagnosed with cancer and given a couple of months to live, the time ahead of me shrank to what seemed like a momentary flash. That's when I adopted the philosophy that early is on time. Now I value every minute.

Don't forget about prep time; factor that in. I'm a known stickler for being on time. When we're off for a run at 9 A.M., that means we hit the road at nine o'clock, which means you need to arrive early enough to tend to your bike and what else you need to get straight for the journey ahead. This all sounds so elementary, I'm almost embarrassed to include it in this book. But you'd be surprised. Time is a funny thing. The older and more experienced you get, the quicker time passes. The more successful you become, the more precious a commodity time becomes. Guard your time from the time wasters and the losers who are apt to bog you down.

The better my bike runs, the quicker time passes. When I'm broken down along the highway under the hot Arizona sun, time slows down. Being consistently on time says a lot about you. It's an easy way to distinguish yourself as dependable in a sea of mediocre people who treat time (like freedom) cheaply, with disdain, and with little regard for its value.

15 Just Talking Never Gets the Job Done

You're at your best when what you think, what you say, and what you do are all in sequential harmony.

If someone wants to ride, hang out, or do business with me, the more transparent he is, the better we get along. The more "think," the less "talk," and the more "do," even better. If you're a good listener, then you've got the complete package. Your actions reveal your truest intentions. I always try to be that one-in-a-thousand person whose actions match his words.

Most people I know, especially motorcycle riders, always have their bullshit detectors set to the max. It seems that anyone who gabs a lot doesn't get far. I've seen it a million times in bars or out on the road. Somebody is scared or gets loaded. Spews a bunch of bullshit. A dozen glances are exchanged. Nobody's buying a bunch of words. All words, no action, no credibility.

You know when you're talking shit and you also know when you're keeping it real. Catch yourself when it's the former. Stop. Strive for the latter. Stop and listen to yourself. I remember one particular person who started out as a bit of a motormouth. The guy talked nonstop bullshit chatter. I could see the guys getting sick of him. I saw the fists clenching and the glances being exchanged. I knew the guy was a gnat's eyelash away from getting his ass kicked. So I took him aside and grabbed him by the throat.

"You need to go to Words Anonymous. Think about what you're going to say first, then cut it in half." (An old writer's trick.)

And it worked. He learned to tone his shit down a little and let his actions say their piece. All I had to do was point the way a little. He's doing fine now, and is a valuable part of the team, second to none among motorcycle mechanics. I saved him from getting lit up, and now, as a result, I get my oil changed for free.

When we have personal problems, nine times out of ten, we know the answer. But that requires thinking about it before we go ask somebody for advice or assistance. Simple rule: "do it" instead of talking about it. You'll see more results and you skip a whole step (the talking part) in the process.

16 There Is No Reverse Gear on a Motorcycle

What a lot of people don't understand about my friends and me is that we spend so much time on our bikes that the mechanics of motorcycling have seeped into our physical and spiritual beings. It's how we think and operate on and off the bike. I've taken on many of the characteristics of my bike. I like to keep moving ahead, quickly. I rarely look back at the miles I've covered; I concentrate instead on the road before me. I split lanes to get ahead faster. I jump off the line quickly when I start. I overheat. I seldom, if ever, operate in reverse.

Since there's no reverse gear on a motorcycle, there's no reverse gear inside me. I don't back down, nor do I retreat and retrace my steps. Instead of regret, I set my mind on forward-oriented goals. I'm a "destination rider," meaning I cover as much ground and miles of territory as quickly as possible. I ride ahead with determination, and unless I'm stopping for food, fuel, or a brief rest, I'm covering maximum ground at maximum speed. I've had a lot of riders comment that keeping up with me on the highway isn't exactly easy.

Have you been around people who dwell on the past, who are stuck on the good or bad times from another era? A real estate deal they should have made, a woman they should have married, the job they didn't take. Sure you have. They are going in reverse big-time.

One of the foremost incidents I remember was a concert featuring the Rolling Stones at the Altamont Speedway in the late 1960s. It, of course, was covered by all sorts of media who called it the end of the hippie era or the Age of Aquarius or something to that effect. The subject still comes up today. People are still looking for answers and still have questions. To me, it was just another bike event. A new decade was on the horizon for me, an era that was to make Altamont seem like a garden party. But enough of that, it's all in the rearview mirror.

Do you know people who won't let you forget the mistakes you made ages ago? That's exactly how your competition and your adversaries want you to think. Disappoint them. Don't even consider going into reverse. Rather than brooding and letting your self-esteem go down the tubes, be on to your next job, caper, scam, brainstorm, or idea. Forget the past, get back on that motorcycle in your mind, and move out on the road and into high gear as quickly as possible. Move forward.

17

Cut Down on
Criminals by
Cutting Down
on Laws

The whole concept of drug "abuse" today has expanded and been redefined. A whole new drug culture has emerged. It seems the entire world now is a self-medicating society. In England, traces of Prozac are showing up in the water supply. Besides illegal street drugs, we now have huge corporations "cranking out" prescription and mood-altering drugs that promise users they can solve their problems of depression and hopelessness simply by popping a pill. In jail they dispense what they term *hot meds.* Recreational usage aside, the entire world has slipped into a conveniently medicated state.

And yet the prisons today are filled with drug-related criminals.

Every day, teenagers in the ghettos are getting busted for peddling nickel bags of weed or crack. And they are doing it just to survive. They're obeying the laws of the streets, and the cops who bust the little guys who are dealing are filling the prisons with these first-time offenders. Once someone young gets thrown in prison, it is hard for them to escape getting sucked into the vortex of crime. They grow up in prison and that's all they know.

But these same cops aren't scouring the beaches at the Club Meds or the swimming pools at the country clubs for the prescribed drug users. They are too busy filling the jails with the poor. Solution?

There are a lot of them, but the simplest one would be to abolish the drug laws altogether. Everyone would be equal and a lot of cops would be out of work. It is my belief that drug usage under a new system with no laws would not go up any more than it is today and would probably even go down.

18 If You're Gonna Gonna Ride, Wear Leather

If you choose to experiment with substances, make sure you know that if you continue with them, at some point the chemicals will be in control and you won't. And losing control is not where anyone wants to be.

Back in the early days of the psychedelic experience of the sixties, before acid was illegal, street chemists and friends liked to test their stuff out on different people. What happens if you take the blue pill with the red one? How good is this dose of acid? How easy does a swig of "Oakland Dew" go down? How potent is this weed? How much can you handle?

At the time, my friends and companions would try anything, once. That's how we were able to test our own limits. For instance, I knew that speed wired me too much. That pot made me hungry. That alcohol made me a greater danger to myself while riding my bike. That reds put me to sleep. That acid was fantastic. That cocaine, besides stealing my soul . . . well, never mind. We'll cover that ground elsewhere.

The 1960s were an era of experimentation, and some of us were there at the beginning. But then the drugs got wider and wider distribution and started moving into the colleges and suburbs. When that started happening it took some of the fun out of it; it was almost coming to the point of legality. It wasn't just something being used by those outside the bounds of society.

Two chemicals blatantly kicked open the doors of freedom for me. The first one is an easy guess. Acid. Not since I began riding motorcycles had any one experience opened up the concept of freedom to me wider than my first trips on acid. There's a lot of truth to the old axiom that if you can remember the sixties, chances are you weren't there. While I do remember those days, the ultimate acid experience is almost impossible to put into words. The world slowed down and magnified. Colors that were deeply embedded in my psyche rushed to the surface. Sound, especially music, became extravagant. A trickle in the gutter resonated like a roaring waterfall.

I have to be honest. Acid expanded my definition of freedom. It became clear to me, for better or worse, that my physical body limited my perception of the physical world. Pure acid jarred loose those physical restrictions and enhanced sounds, smells, and colors. Of course some of us went overboard. We made the party we had created into a shipwreck. The mixture of acid and my friends on motorcycles wasn't always a good one. But for me, I respected the drug's power and I've never regretted a single trip I took. I've seen people ride out some real bummers, and I helped them get through them, but for me, acid was an interesting, entertaining, and smooth ride inward.

I bring this up for the benefit of the young. Remember that as far as chemicals are concerned, you have choices. First, you need to be cautious, even more cautious than we were back in our early days. The majority of the people in prison right now are there as a result of bad choices, alcohol, and drugs. The authorities are on the watch. There are a lot more laws now than existed forty years ago.

While I enjoyed LSD, which opened up a new world to me, I also fell in love with cocaine, which put me in prison and cost me dearly in terms of my freedom.

Some people say they don't ride motorcycles because they are too dangerous. They are—just like drugs. It is your responsibility to know this in the first place. You have to be alert, you have to be prepared, and it doesn't hurt to wear leather so if you take a spill you won't scrape the skin off your body.

A big part of my freedom today is being free from any dependency.

As just an aside, I've adopted my own personal

campaign and that is against cigarette smoking. Rather than calling for more laws telling people what to do, I've taken it upon myself to deal with it on a much more effective and personal one-on-one level.

At book signings and personal appearances, whenever a small kid walks up with his parents, to the table where I'm signing, I lean over and ask, "Know why I talk this way?," putting my thumb over the plastic valve in my throat that enables me to speak since I lost my voice box.

Invariably, the kid, scared, shakes his head.

"Because I smoked cigarettes," I tell them. "So promise me you won't smoke cigarettes."

Then we shake hands on the deal.

The parents, standing behind, look pleased. And I've done my part to try to rob the tobacco companies of one more sucker customer.

All in a day's work.

To sum up, all of this drug abuse, addiction, medication, and prescription is a form of hiding from and avoiding the real world and the real you. Be in charge is the name of the game in my book, being prepared is my credo, and substances . . . they just get in the way.

19 Customize Yourself. Originals Don't Come Off the Assembly Line.

Don't be so damned run-of-the-mill and buttoned down. There are already enough scared people out there occupying the middle of the road and afraid to show their colors or speak their minds.

There was a time when motorcycle riders were looked on as total outcasts. There were so few bikes on the road, we bike riders waved at one another when we crossed paths on the streets and highways. That's when bike culture was custom and each bike was a one-of-a-kind. We built them (or should I say rebuilt them?) in our garages with our bare hands, adding our own signature touches. Even today, when we are regarded as acceptable outcasts, our motorcycles can still reflect a rider's self-image. Millions are enthralled with the mystical process of building customized motorcycles as seen on television reality shows.

The motorcycle started out as a far simpler (and cheaper) machine than the car—as a vehicle that almost anyone could ride, fix, or rebuild. Men prided themselves

on doing their own work and expressing themselves through the individual nuances of their choppers. Whether it was with paint and chrome, forging our own parts (like we often had to do), or adding after-market accessories, we found a hell of a lot of ways to personalize a Harley so that it reflects its owner. The same process applies to customizing yourself.

Here are a couple of things to remember in customizing yourself. A lot of bikes today have little or no appeal to me because they're unrideable. They may look nice at a bike show. They might sparkle and shine in your garage (or in a living room, where a few of my more obsessive friends keep their bikes). They might even look beautiful arranged inside a museum like the Guggenheim in New York City. But unfortunately, most show bikes are hell to take out on the highway for a casual spin. They're hard to keep on the road, they break down, they are hard to drive, and they're simply dangerous. You have to trailer them to get from Point A to Point B. Beneath all the glitz and glamour, you need to have substance. They need to work. Are you getting my drift? Underneath the "bike," the clothes and the accessories, who and where's the real man or woman?

An important thing to remember is that when you take a stock bike and add to it or customize it, it not only looks cooler and rides faster, it automatically becomes less dependable and maintainable. It may no longer be under its warranty. That doesn't mean you shouldn't beef up a bike, or yourself for that matter. It just means, once you begin the customizing process, expect to spend more time on maintenance. The process is ongoing.

That said, Harley-Davidson and other organizations have built empires and billion-dollar corporations based on designs that riders like us, as yesterday's outcasts, invented years ago. There was a time during the sixties and seventies when we rode rigid-framed chops, and Harley-Davidson dealers chased us out of their stores. Our old ladies had to buy all our parts because the dealers wouldn't sell them to us. By adapting their product to our own needs, we were, in their eyes, messing with the basic designs of Harley-Davidson. Again, we were considered the one percent giving ninety-nine percent of the other motorcycles a bad name. Once we got our hands on a new bike, we immediately stripped it down to its bare essentials and rebuilt it from the ground up. Now those same stripping ideas, once considered bad, are mainstream concepts. Chopped frames are the norm, while other innovations, such as ape-hangers, smaller seats, tiny peanut gas tanks, louder pipes, and other radical engine modifications that we pioneered, have made the bikes of today run faster and look way cooler.

The bad part today is that with all the modern electronic technology, it's more difficult to perform your own emergency roadside maintenance on a contemporary Harley. You now need a nearby shop—and guess what?—they exist, everywhere. Even small towns now have Harley shops. That's how much our tiny innovations shook and changed an entire marketplace.

Here's the lesson. First, customize yourself and don't be afraid to go the whole hog. Don't be afraid to step out and be different. I emphasize taking the road less traveled, whether you're on a run or navigating your way through life. It's a vital theme that bears consideration. You don't need to be a bike rider, an actor, an athlete, or a musician in order to be different. I've known doctors who drove race cars. I've known auto mechanics who flew airplanes. I've known bankers who raced horses. I've known teachers who raised snakes. Part of being free is deviating from the norm or simply being yourself.

If you're going to customize yourself, during the process of rebuilding yourself, make sure you retain a sense of practicality. Remember the lesson about the bike that looked great but rode like shit. In your quest to be unique, don't turn yourself into an unrideable show bike that can't make it two blocks down the street. As you begin to challenge the norm, remember what we experienced rebuilding our motorcycles and pissing off Harley-Davidson. Radical ideas (especially those with the right form and function) are eventually swallowed up and adopted by the mainstream. Yesterday's object of ridicule and scorn, whether it's riding a motorcycle or selling bottled water, is often tomorrow's brilliant mainstream idea. Yesterday's revolutionary act can easily become today's middle-of-the-road behavior. But keep moving forward, because if everyone is alternative, then no one is.

If it's happened in almost every field—politics, business, art, motorcycles, and cars—why not make it happen to you?

20 Only One Person Can Ride a Motorcycle

It's not a good idea to mess with another man's woman. To me, that's always been a given.

I've seen men get shot over women; I've seen women get shot over men. Love is the world's oldest and most fought-over situation. Men are always wondering what women are thinking, women are always trying to second-guess men. But the no-no, the line you don't cross, is coming between two people who are a unit.

Mess with another man's money. Cheat at cards. Steal his motorcycle. Those are all "hanging offenses." But messing with another person's partner creates the worst tornadoes of all. It messes up a lot of people on a whole lot of levels. Don't do it and don't tolerate it. Nip it in the bud. It's a cancer. Cut it out. Strike another match. It'll only spread and kill you from the inside out.

We count on our friends to do their part to keep their family problems out of others' affairs. If a wife or old lady (or a son or daughter, for that matter) is the source of trouble that affects you or your organization, look to that person to control the situation. I've had old ladies that were shining examples and I've had old ladies that were completely out of control. Believe me, it isn't easy. I've had to cut loose from women who were unable to walk the line and conduct themselves properly.

A good leader leads by example. If I don't keep myself straight, it's hard to expect another man within my group to keep himself straight. If I can't control my own household, who else is going to? Relationships can be a constant source of drama and headache. No matter how valuable someone might be, if they can't keep it together on the home front, they're not all that valuable. On the contrary, they're a liability.

As long as you're dealing with people, you can only hope that the smartest ones will have the common sense to keep their affairs and domestic crises out of the way of others. It's a simple matter, so to speak, of the separation of church and state.

21 Gonna Take a Beating? Hell, No, Fight Back.

I believe in the luck of the draw, not some predetermined destiny. Then I push my luck further.

I've had lots of people come up to me, shake my hand, pat me on the back, and tell me how much they admire me because I cheated death by whipping cancer. As if anybody's capable of whipping cancer. I considered it my destiny to live on.

When cancer attacked my body, specifically my throat, and I was diagnosed after a life spent smoking nonfiltered Camel cigarettes, I was handed a death sentence: two months to live, tops. The doctors sent me packing. Don't even bother to quit smoking, they said. I was a goner.

I'd seen a lot of death, and a lot of riders will tell you, death is part of the script when you ride a motorcycle. Close friends may be here today, gone by Friday. You get to know how tenuous life really is by just riding a motorcycle down the street. You live with the fact that all it takes is the slightest turn of somebody's steering wheel or the smallest pothole or scrap of rubber in the road, and the next thing you know, you could be playing checkers upstairs with William Harley and Arthur Davidson. You accept death's odds by knowing that life is a volatile balance of good and bad luck. In Johnny Cash's words, you walk the line.

In my case, the doctors were wrong, dead wrong. I even outlived a few of them. Twenty-three years later, I'm still here, still ridin'. I attribute part of that longevity to the fact that I was too stubborn to give up, too pissed off to stop lifting weights and staying strong. But also, my luck turned. My advice is to not give up, just in case the doctors don't really know and you are that one-in-a-thousand case that proves them all wrong. I'm using my story as an example.

It would be easy, out of conceit, for me to lead you on and tell you that I miraculously cheated death by beating cancer. But I didn't. I lived. Nobody's god from out of the sky saved me or struck me down. Rather, my lymph nodes did their job by absorbing the toxins, saving my life. Listen to your body. I'm still around because I did. My body fought back, telling me it wasn't my time. My meter hadn't run out. Yet.

Your body is an amazing machine. If you take even

marginally good care of it, it'll bounce back when attacked. If you've smoked for a lifetime, take a few years off the weed and chances are your body and lungs can shake off the effects of nicotine by returning to close to normal. By eating well and spending time in the gym, even with cancer hanging over you, given the miraculous way the human body is constructed and functions, you stand a chance of rebounding and leading a longer life, if you're lucky.

Cancer used to be considered a death sentence. As with RICO, people would just hear the word and throw in the towel. Not so much anymore. Destiny—which I don't believe in—or "life" (as I like to call it) can be improved on by a man's own proactive determination and free will. Rather than merely praying, or waiting for the right roll of the dice, get out there and lose weight, eat less poisonous food, and suffer through that extra round of exercise even when it seems impossible. That's what's going to save your life. That and your mind's determination.

Until your meter runs out, live to cheat death for another day. There's more at your disposal and command than you might initially suspect. Even if the roof caves in, don't automatically give up. Don't miss a golden opportunity to save yourself by waiting for a miracle that's not going to happen. It may be up to you, a test only you can pass.

22

If You Can't Change the Players, Then Change the Game

Are you outgunned and outnumbered?
Change the shape and perception of the battlefield.

When I was in grade school, we all put our hands on our hearts and recited the Pledge of Allegiance to the flag, ending with the words "with liberty and justice for all." It sounded good to me, an excellent concept, though I'm not really sure I believed liberty and justice really existed for all of us. The government I pledged allegiance to then was to become my foe later. At one point, I frequently fought with the feds at every turn and corner. With its unlimited resources, the government became a formidable opponent. I was a small and outgunned individual limited to what legal weapons I had to fire back with. I was forced to figure out a way to beat the odds and slay the giant with a single stone.

If it's liberty and justice and a fair fight you're after, and if you're going to be a player inside the criminal justice system, or any other competitive arena or organization, you need to get good at playing, or at least at changing the perception of the game.

I was the first motorcycle rider in Oakland to own a Harley Sportster. At the time, they were considered sport bikes, starter bikes, or even ladies' bikes. But I found them to be quicker, lighter, easy to ride, hotter off the line, and a better bike to race and dodge enemies and the cops on.

The point of this example is that you have to learn what the rules are, interpret them, and then use them to your benefit. Sport bikes were legal, I knew how to ride mine better, and I managed to beat the system and my opponents.

Maybe you've got legal problems. Problems with your old lady. Business hassles. You're ready to pack it in, because according to those around you, the odds are royally stacked against you.

I've been up against the most aggressive opponents one man could face. It was "us," a small group of guys, against the vast resources of "them," the United States government. These were dark times, when we were constantly in and out of jail and court, fighting desperately for our freedom. It looked for a while as if we might lose our footing under all the extreme pressure. Friends and allies lost faith. But those who remained were the best of the team. We learned and abided by the rules and stayed strong. We reviewed our situation for what it really was—a game, a contest, and a match. By indicting us, the cops may have won the first rounds in the press. We were in jail. No bail. But the game was far from over. We had to go to court.

Consequently, we put together the right team of people, people willing to go the distance by remaining flexible if things needed adjustment, but also willing to follow a leader and stick to our proven and predetermined course of action.

A brainy defense can often outfox a brawny offense. Just like my sport bike could outrun my enemies'. Instead of presenting tons of charts, witnesses, and evidence that bored the jury, we turned our courtroom into a game show. At the time, competition on the raceway came more naturally to me than competition in the courtroom. I figured we needed speed and ingenuity. We were the objects of yet another multidefendant trial designed to wear us down and pulverize us. But by turning a critically grave situation into a contest, we gained a more competitive edge, and ultimately the advantage, and we won the game.

23 Don't Listen to "Them" Whoever "They" Are

Over and over we hear the phrases "If they would only . . ." or "That's what they say." Who is this "they" that people are constantly referring to? Those at the top? The politicians? The rich? The intelligent? Or is it the authorities?

I've fought authority and authority isn't always right and doesn't always win.

By definition, authority isn't going to encourage anybody to change things. Most of us were brought up with the notion of respecting authority, that the policeman on the corner was our friend, that the government we pay for is out to serve and protect us, that, as a result, as Americans, we will remain free. We also are taught that judges impartially interpret the law. That if you work hard, your boss and your company will stand firmly behind your efforts. These are the authority figures most of us deal with throughout our lives. These are the "they" people I am referring to. However you choose to handle authority, don't let it deter you from maintaining your own self-reliant vision.

Rarely in the history of this country has it been harder to get something new off the ground than it is today. But it's not impossible. We are now a nation hamstrung by more rules, regulations, and special interests than ever before. It may seem that those who prosper are those who stick closest to the tried and trusted formulas, who stay close to home, who play it safe and are resistant to innovation. But I don't believe it. I never have.

If you want to do something, go ahead and try it. That's how the first airplanes and automobiles were born, by breaking the rules, defying the status quo, and persisting in a dream. So if you want to start a new venture, expect the banks, accountants, attorneys, and the reigning competition (they, them, the authorities) to tell you what you can't or shouldn't do. Then do it anyway.

If you're looking for the next innovative idea, don't listen to the folks sitting comfortably at the top of the heap. Check out the people at the bottom, who are hungry and are tirelessly, slowly, and steadily working their way upward. These are the people who have a far clearer view of the battlefield, the reality.

In your process of creation, be careful who you write off. All sorts of everyday people have started revolutions and movements. Tired old ladies on buses in Selma have inspired revolutions. Misfit awkward nerds like Gandhi changed the course of the British Empire. Guys who couldn't get a date on Saturday night as teenagers have started billion-dollar software corporations. The works of painters who died penniless and unpopular are now auctioned for millions.

Listen to yourself and believe in what you want and not what you think they want. Take on the competition; you alone can make the world a better place, but only if "you," not "they," want to.

24

Knowledge Is Out There, but It Don't Come Served to You on a Bun

Admit to yourself when you're in the dark. Don't go on fumbling around in it, acting like a tough guy or, worse yet, the smart guy.

There's nothing wrong with saying the three simple words: *I don't know.*

If you don't know, say so. Better yet, ask. Even better, learn. Lots of times it is pure arrogance that drives us. You fake it, someone else fakes it, and after a while you start to wonder who is kidding whom. Time spent wandering around lost could have been time spent learning what it was you didn't know in the first place. Sounds basic, I know. What I don't understand is why so many people just can't say, "I don't know."

I'll only give one small example because I think you get my drift.

Once I was going to the Sturgis rally in South Dakota and I had been forewarned that there might be some trouble from the other clubs. I knew I was outnumbered, but I also knew I could fight back with everything I had, no matter what the cost. I started thinking of something or some way I could be one up on the opposition. Then I asked around. When I was told about a certain law in South Dakota, I went and made sure that it was indeed still in force. It was, but with one wrinkle. It was a gun law that said you had to register all loaded guns before you entered a certain area. Instead of turning them in, you just had to unload them. It still created an illusion of power. You could wear as many guns as you wanted, all exposed and everything, but felons (as I was later to become) could not carry guns. The law separated the sheep from the goats, the felons from the nonfelons, in other words, and the NFers went strapped like warriors, with almost every firearm imaginable. The opposition never showed their faces. If I hadn't asked earlier on, gotten a tip, and followed up on it, things in South Dakota that year might have been very different.

Knowledge, some wise man once said, is power and it's up to you to go and seek it and use it to your advantage.

Only the arrogant remain ignorant.

25 Learn from the Past, Don't Live There

Don't dwell on your bad experiences from the past. They come at a high cost. Value them. Bank them.

As I get older, in nearly every interview, I'm asked about regrets. Do I have any? I have three that come to mind, which is far fewer than most people. *Regret* is a word whose meaning has been distorted and watered down. So when I say "regrets," I'm talking about key actions and events that I've paid and taken responsibility for.

My first regret is having smoked cigarettes. Cigarettes are clearly one of the most deadly products produced and mass-marketed in this country. They are habit-forming, over-the-counter drugs that up until recently were the products of advertisements that sold lifestyle. Since tobacco is legally grown in eighteen states of the Union, it is an integral part of our economy. It was one of the first cash crops grown when we were just thirteen colonies. But even though I don't like tobacco and choose not to use it, I believe Americans who enjoy the habit should be free to smoke wherever and whenever they wish. By the same token, though, they should take stock and responsibility for the hospital bills and the health costs that result from their behavior. Not to mention the high cost of cigarettes themselves.

My second regret is that as a result of doing time in prison and because I'd done too much cocaine, I lost my right to vote and bear arms. I hold the Second Amendment in the highest esteem, and I regret no longer having the right to carry a gun in order to defend my freedom and myself.

My final regret is having done too much cocaine during the sixties and the seventies. While I found coke to be far less addictive than cigarettes, it was way too expensive. For almost three years, it was my drug of choice. I loved it so much, I sold it to finance my own personal use. (At least I was smart enough not to become a heroin junkie.) I could spend days, sometimes weeks, binging on cocaine. I had the freedom and at the time I knew exactly what I was doing, which was enjoying myself to excess. At the time I was a user, there were no such things as celebrity clinics and rehab centers designed to wean users off drugs through a steady treatment and support program. You either took a twelve-step program, stopped cold turkey, quit in jail, checked into a nuthouse, or died broke. I've been hooked on coke and I've been hooked on cigarettes. Cigarettes were a much harder habit to kick. It took the first days in prison for me to stop doing cocaine. It took one day of surgery to stop smoking. Both could be considered extreme cures.

We all live with our own separate and unique regrets and I've willingly paid the price for most of my mistakes. Dwelling on and feeling remorse about my regrets don't do much good. Learning from them is the only thing you really can do. Do yourself a big favor. Put your regrets in the rearview mirror where they belong, ride away, and don't look back.

26 Truth Is the Ball Breaker

Either testifying in court or conveying a simple message to someone intelligently means arriving prepared, with your facts straight and your presentation organized. I don't advocate walking into any situation or meeting unprepared or, more important, not properly prepped and coached by the people around you who are in the know. I've lived my life trying to be honest and straightforward with everybody. Making the transition into a courtroom or a boardroom, or anywhere for that matter, isn't that difficult if you have, as they say, your ducks in a row.

But here's the kicker in your presentation. Tell the whole truth, warts and all. There's nothing more convincing than someone who speaks truthfully, who tells the whole tale, the good, the bad, and the ugly. Being truthful about both the bad and the good lends credibility to your argument. Look people in the eye when you speak to them because they will be looking back at you and judging your honesty.

And this especially goes for relationships. Both men and women like it served straight up—the whole truth and nothing but the truth, so help me . . .

It's a winding road, so you have to be honest with yourself about the strengths and weaknesses of your presentation. I can tell if I'm getting my message across to someone by watching them carefully and gauging their reactions to the things I've said. Can you? If your presentation was filmed or taped, could you objectively step back and evaluate yourself honestly? If it was a movie or a book, would you root for yourself?

No matter how much I may differ culturally from whoever it is I'm trying to persuade, I can always relate to someone who has the courage and good sense to speak up and/or listen for themselves, take responsibility for all their actions, good and bad, instead of ducking and hiding behind silence. That only leads to speculation. What is that person hiding?

I ended up winning one of my court cases by convincing the jury that yes, I wasn't a murderer. By having my attorney lead me into a lot of details about my life and my many transgressions, the jury found my entire story credible partly because I had prepared my testimony extensively by going over each and every detail over and over. My delivery and my message were clear and not muddled. I answered with confidence the questions that were posed to me. I was easy to understand and relate to, and by simply telling the truth, I even came across as sympathetic.

Whenever you have the luxury of telling your own story, I recommend it, because time and time again, I've found that being well prepared and presenting the truth always wins.

27 Nothing States Your Position More Clearly Than a Punch in the Face

Fighting and brawling are believed to be means of expression reserved for gangsters, outlaws, and, well, motorcycle riders. I plead guilty to that. Yet I maintain that you're unlikely to find a more invigorating and exhausting barroom pursuit than fighting. Fighting is physically demanding, and is a severe test of courage and fortitude. It can be the best way to settle an argument. One thing you have to remember about a good, honest fistfight is that at its best, it's conclusive, and if you score a knockout, it is final.

I'm not talking about gunplay, knives, or back-alley techniques (though all of those things have their own time and place); I'm talking about mano a mano fisticuffs. It's a dying art in most circles, though not in mine. Many a dispute is settled with our fists, whether it's caused by someone who's had a bit too much to drink and is running his mouth, or by someone who is out to prove their willingness to stand up for themselves, or whether it has to do with an incident stemming from a basic (but temporary) lack of respect.

Fistfighting is a direct and spontaneous form of conflict resolution. It's sad that it's not utilized in business and political circles today. Think of the lives and money that might be saved if our leaders duked it out among themselves. They would get younger, quick. Basically, all conflicts could be averted and settled with only a few quick punches. While fighting has its violent repercussions, it's the best way to clear the air. For those few seconds or minutes, it no longer matters who you are, what car you drive, what you do for a living, or how much money you make. On the streets of modern America, all that should matter is how tough and tenacious you are and how willing you are to stand up for what you believe and say.

Fighting is quick and right to the point. It requires a physical sacrifice, and since pain is involved, it forces people to pick the arguments they truly care about. It also solves a situation quickly and definitively.

Unarmed fighting is an overlooked art and a noble science. It can be your most complete and mobile self-defense system. Bare-fist fighting need not be considered a crude activity practiced by criminals and thugs. European martial arts utilize different styles and techniques. There are closed-fist, open-hand, elbow, and arm techniques. There are also kicking, sweeping, and knee techniques, not to mention head butting. Once two opponents hit the ground, there's grappling and wrestling. The biggest brawls I've fought have lasted a couple of minutes, tops. The greatest fighters are those who really know how to jump in fast and turn out the lights quickly, using a variety of fighting skills. These are the guys you want on your side if and when the room turns against you.

Granted, all this sounds over-the-top. The point I'm trying to make is that we should strongly consider bringing back the more physical aspects of problem solving. Instead of hiring a lawyer to take care of our conflicts, why not solve disagreements physically, by fighting, wrestling, arm wrestling, whatever physical activity will get the job done? Aaron Burr and Alexander Hamilton dueled with pistols and they were both lawyers! Physicality involves sacrifice, and if you are willing to sacrifice to win your case and get your point across, then this idea of mine has some merit for you.

I see people solving too many of their disputes with costly and timely litigation (so much time goes by that the passion is gone and you can forget about what the problem was in the first place) and paperwork. Lots of paperwork, with the proper documents having to be filed, stamped, approved, and so forth. At the end of the day, something may be resolved, but the real winners are the lawyers. They walk away with wheelbarrows of cash. I've talked to a lot of lawyers, and even they're tired of all the paperwork and bullshit. The worst part of their job, they claim, is dealing with other lawyers.

Let's bring back the more simple and direct elements of problem solving. The good old-fashioned fist-fight.

28 You Can't Appoint, Hire, or Declare Leadership

I've heard athletic team captains say that they garner much more respect from their teammates if the team chooses them as a captain than if the coach appoints them. You are not a true leader until you're perceived as a leader by your own people, and not by an executive proclamation. No title or promotion or appointment is going to give you, as a leader, the respect you need in order to make your people forget their own limits, accomplish goals beyond those limits, and do everything possible to succeed together as an organization.

Take, for example, the leaders in various countries. Royalty are those born into their positions as kings and queens. Do the people, the working classes, really respect the leadership of those kings and queens? Notice how a lot of these countries regard their royalty as just figureheads and grant them little or no power to rule.

Titles don't make the man.

Being a leader is a hassle. An important thing I've

learned about leadership is that just like the rank and file, leaders need constant guidance and motivation. If you are someone a leader can fully trust and fall back on, take some time to motivate them. By doing this, you'll find yourself playing an enormously important role in shaping a winning organization.

The best leadership is accomplished by achieving honor and dignity, by becoming a role model. I hear that a lot and it's true. Leadership isn't just a matter of ordering and bullying people around. A leader must be an organizer. A planner. A persuader. A person of confidence, a person with self-esteem.

Leadership arises more from how others perceive you than from how you perceive yourself.

29 Take a Pit Stop, Overhaul Your Psyche

Some call it soul-searching. I call it taking inventory. Every now and then, make a pit stop so you can pause and objectively take stock of yourself and your life.

People view motorcycle riders as being strong, decisive, and confident. Women fall hard for men on bikes because they sense both inner and outer strength. They perceive that we're a determined lot and that we know what we want out of life. (Well, they are right!)

No matter how old you are, I believe that all of us have the potential to be tougher and smarter than we were yesterday. But first, you've got to take time out in order to take stock, to figure out what parts of your body and mind might need tuning up. Every so often, our bodies, like our machines, need careful adjustment and maintenance. We might not be in the right groove. We may regularly do a diagnostic check on our bikes, but do we do it to ourselves?

Over twenty years ago, I was on the road to smoking myself to death. I needed to stop and take a breather, but I wouldn't. I was too stubborn. Fortunately, my friends intervened. By looking death in the face after being diagnosed with throat cancer, I chose the option of reinventing my body and brain into a finely tuned machine as opposed to an abused receptacle for nicotine, booze, and drugs. While I was strong, willing, and able to kick ass, my physical and mental attitudes were not in concert. My mind was saying one thing (*Oh, go ahead, you only live once . . .*) while my body was saying something different (*You'd better slow down, kiddo . . .*). By making the commitment to live a healthier lifestyle, eating better, working out more regularly, staying fit, and quitting cigarettes, I took a necessary course of action.

Over the years, we all slip a little in the strength-training department. I find it harder to make smart decisions if I'm physically off-kilter. How far off the mark have you physically let yourself go? Shaping up is a process anyone can take on. There are effective strength-building programs and diets out there adjusted to your age, weight, and physical needs and limitations. I know, because I once owned a gym. Fitness was my trade, and it's remained an obsession.

With physical strength comes mental sharpness. I also find emotional health to be the immediate and natural by-product of being in better physical shape.

Self-confidence paves the way for the long-term goals you need to accomplish. Aggressive physical conditioning is like staying sober; it's an ongoing process, not just a day's decision. No guru or religious leader told me this. I learned and experienced it for myself.

As part of a tune-up and inventory process, I recommend you turn off the television, pick up a book, work those mental muscles, and exercise that flabby imagination inside your head. Television eats time and tends to suck people into an imaginary world of idiotic priorities. Next, take a couple of weeks (or months) off the alcohol and substances. See what happens. Feel what it's like to have a clearer head on top of a lighter, stronger body.

There are more than six billion people on Earth today and what did you do to make a difference? What did you do in material terms? What about something you did for someone else? Finally, did you set an example for someone other than yourself? Never write yourself off.

After you get your body in shape, jump on your motorcycle (or whatever it is that keeps your heart pumping), and take a 360-degree look at your world. For at least a day, stop living mindlessly, according to your routines and habits. Think about what you're doing, eating, and how you're spending your last few precious units of time on Earth. For an entire day, become hypersensitive to your surroundings and see if you can't remember what attracted you to this particular time and space, your environment, in the first place. Why are you still here? You might have a lot of reasons to stick around. Your old lady. Your job. Your family. Your friends. Yourself. If you can't think of a single good reason to continue down the road you're riding, then you might consider radically changing your direction, wiping the slate clean, and beginning anew someplace else. It's difficult but sometimes necessary.

For me, it all started with a few minor adjustments, a tune-up, a simple inventory, and then a cold, hard look at my daily routine. By completely taking stock, you're less apt to do something you'll regret later on down the line.

30 Be Careful Writing People Off. They Can Be Rebuilt.

If a "basket case" falls into your lap, can you spot its hidden potential?

One of the best things about old Harleys is that they're virtually indestructible. Old Harleys don't die; they just go on to become what I call basket cases. There is still something usable but not in the same form. A once-proud classic Harley, after years of wear and tear, neglect, or abuse, is reduced to a box of parts. On the surface, it's a pathetic sight, a bike in a box. But if you develop an eye for motorcycle potential, you can see past a basket of parts and visualize the find of the century. Short of a complete meltdown, you can rebuild damn near any Harley-Davidson. You just have to be clever enough to spot a motorcycle's potential.

I've known people who have paid thousands for a basket case because they were able to see that, from the rubble and parts, a vintage rigid frame or a rebuilt classic police bike was waiting to emerge. A bent and rusted frame, the core and foundation of a solid motorcycle, can usually be straightened. It's not easy, but with a veteran frame straightener, the results can be miraculous. Forks, swing arms, pivot bolts, steering stops, and distorted head stocks can be repaired and brought back up to factory service specs. A competent frame straightener can perform most of these services so that, upon completion, they are virtually undetectable. No cuts, grind marks, or obtrusive welds, just a smooth, sleek, and restored frame upon which to restore your bike.

Then there's the cosmetic angle to consider because that is what people will see first. Your look. A new paint job can be as elaborate as a showpiece with flames, stripes, graphics, and even murals painted over the original base coat onto the tank and fenders. Or you can take the simpler route, with something as clean, plain, and undetectable as a brand-new stock paint job.

It's the same case with people. You'll be surprised what you can create today among society's castoffs, rejects, and basket cases. If I can see character and toughness in someone, especially if they have true grit, maybe they're worth restoring, investing time in, or virtually rebuilding.

In the past, when some friends were released from prison, instead of getting a "nonassociation clause" from their parole officers, meaning they're forbidden to associate with bike riders, they got an "association clause."

We weren't the only organization out of Oakland taking chances on people. The Oakland Raiders did the same thing when owner Al Davis created a winning organization from the NFL's collection of rebels and outcasts.

Be extremely cautious in judging and writing people off. If you're dealing with truly unique individuals, be sure you're looking deep enough below the surface to see if there's something salvageable. Of course we can never be a hundred percent sure of a person's true character, so do your due diligence, your homework, and, above all, listen to your gut.

Just because someone might be aggressive, weathered, and rough around the edges doesn't mean they can't learn new tricks or that they're not worthy of another chance at life. Or that through their experiences, they can't teach you a new trick or two about success. If all someone needs is guidance and leadership administered with love and respect—a little straightening, new parts, and a paint job—you might want to take the gamble. Some of my best friends were the same people others considered incorrigible and impossible to deal with. I saw them turn themselves from scrap into a powerful force to be reckoned with. Granted, it's a risky proposition, with lots at stake, but I believe that the greater the risk, the higher the potential for gain.

31 How Strong You Look Is as Important as How Strong You Are

Unfortunately, I'm not much of a poker player. For all the years I've spent in the joint, I haven't played cards all that much. But I've known lots of guys who gamble for a living with a system that they have developed and follow religiously. Since I'm not much of a gambler, I tend to overanalyze and go for the sure bet. But one thing that I have garnered from playing the game is the development of a poker face. When you sit down to do business, having an effective poker face gives you a hell of an advantage.

Power and poker involve keeping those around you guessing, especially during tense play and negotiation. I suppose that's what the game is all about. At the poker table, the strongest players look for the weakest bluffers. What's your strategy in keeping up a strong front, even when you're standing on shaky ground? Whether you're in a courtroom or a conference room, nothing conveys strength like neutrality. A neutral, impassive face with focus and intimidating depth can throw your opponent much more than hard looks, angry words, pounding fists, and idle threats. The person with the most forceful expression generally has the weakest hand.

A poker face is the best screen, blocking out telltale verbal and nonverbal indicators.

A tell is a poker mannerism that identifies your holdings. Smiling when you have a big (very good) hand is an obvious tell. Subtler tells include iris dilations, a throbbing pulse, or acting in a certain manner in a given situation like frowning when you get a bad card.

Most of us have our tells. What's yours? Think about it. Is it smiling, is it frowning, does your interest get piqued or ebb away. We naturally tend to "telegraph" our emotions with expressions and gestures, and they disclose our strengths and weaknesses. A tell hinders your negotiating power and weakens your position.

Sit-downs and negotiations are like poker games. You have interests to protect; otherwise, you wouldn't be playing the game, and the object of the game is to walk away a winner.

Only thirty percent of what is communicated

between two people sitting in front of each other is verbal. The other seventy percent is body language, tone of voice, hesitations, inflections, and pauses. That's why a lot of people hide behind telephones to communicate.

If you're up against a frequent rival, get to know his quirks. It might constitute knowing whether your opponent is holding a good hand or if he's bluffing. Figuring out an opponent's tell is an underrated weapon.

Here are a few hints to maintain an effective poker face that can be used in a lot of situations.

Don't move a lot. Sit still.

Breathe normally. (Under pressure, this is easier said than done.)

A poker face isn't a mean or menacing look, so don't stare intensely.

Don't show your teeth.

Avoid looking smug or self-satisfied. That's a hard look to maintain. If you're winning, or if momentum seems to be shifting toward your side, or if your opponent is on the brink of blinking, don't show it by gloating.

Watch your posture. Slumping is as much of a tell of weakness and defeat as sitting up too straight. The idea is to look neither defeated nor victorious.

The most important thing to learn is how to relax. You might even want to go so far as to practice relaxing your face in the mirror. While you are looking into the mirror, ask yourself, *Is this a guy who is strong?*

Whether you're on trial, making an important business pitch, or buying a new washing machine, the more relaxed you are, the better it will serve you over the long haul. A long sit-down is filled with a lot of boredom interrupted by seconds of horror, fear, or panic. Hang in there and stay cool.

The true masters of body language are judges. I've rarely been able to guess the verdict of any trial based on the thirty seconds between the time the judge glances at the verdict slip he has been handed by the bailiff and the moment of truth when he reads the verdict aloud. In all my days spent on trial, rarely have I seen a good judge tip his hand and give you a clue. Judges have excellent control of their bodies and their emotions, not only during the moments of truth, but also, if they're good, throughout the entire proceedings. Learn from them. It is one of the reasons they appear powerful and in control.

32

Find Your Speed, Maintain Velocity, Keep on Doin' It

I'm on the highway a lot, and I equate living with riding. I've put so many miles on so many motorcycles that nothing—and I mean nothing—I see on the highway surprises me. As age slows my reflexes, the trade-off is that I'm now much wiser on the road. I stay tough, I stay cool, and I leave road rage to the less experienced traveler. The challenge to driving or riding is knowing the simple rules, finding a groove and sticking to it.

I've ridden all over America, and in Europe and Asia, and have found that almost every highway has its own rhythm, pace, and feel. In America, a long desolate central California interstate spanning hundreds of miles feels one way, a beautiful winding road into the mountains of Colorado, Oregon, or Washington State feels another. I've ridden pancake-flat stretches across New Mexico, Arizona, Texas, and Oklahoma, and back roads through the big sky, lakes, and trees of Montana and the Dakotas. I've ridden the landscaped six-lane California freeways and the urban expressways and antiquated turnpikes in Pennsylvania and New Jersey to the elevated waterways at the southernmost tip of Florida. In Japan, I rode the crisscrossed superhighways. In the Swiss Alps, I rode upward through the clouds. I've ridden the highways through France, Germany, Scandinavia, and the British Isles. You hear people say that the world is shrinking, but if you actually hit the highways on a motorcycle, you realize it hasn't shrunk at all. It's as massive as ever. There's a lot to see and experience, there's lots of highway out there. And the highway is my lifeline.

The rules of any two-lane or four-lane highway are simple. The right lane is for cruising. The left lane is the passing lane. It is not intended to be a fast lane. I'll repeat: it is a passing lane. A passing lane is designed for maneuvering around those people who have the right to go slower, just as it's my right to rocket around them if I choose to live life at a faster clip. So to spell it out real simple: You cruise in the right lane. When you come upon a slower vehicle than yourself, you pass them by going into the left lane, then you go back into the right lane. Those are the simple rules. Negotiating the highway successfully starts with knowing your pace in the big picture, either as a leader or a follower, and not as someone obstructing the flow. Which are you?

The highway is designed to accommodate all sorts of travelers, both leaders and followers. Since there are miles and miles of roadway, theoretically there's plenty of space for everyone. By driving willy-nilly at inconstant speeds, idiotic drivers upset the natural flow and balance of the road for everyone. They turn travel into a chaotic and needlessly competitive experience.

I try to find the Zen of the highway and stay constant. Here are a few rules of the road I like to follow that keep me on course.

Find your speed, maintain your velocity, keep it up, keep it consistent, and stay in the pocket. If someone directly ahead of me seems headed in the same direction at the same rate of speed, I might lock in and pace them.

Listen to your vehicle. Very often it's trying to tell you something. As long as I've had AM/FM-radio-equipped Harleys, I can't remember turning one on. I prefer to listen to the sound of my own engines.

Stay alert. Glance frequently at your rearview mirror. Make sure it's clean and unobstructed so that you can identify even the most subtle dangers coming from behind you. Use your wits, and not necessarily your speed. Keep an eye on the open skies and the open road. Be ready for anything.

Most important, stay out of the passing lane except

when you need to pass someone. Travel isn't a race. If you're leading, find the right speed and pace that accommodates the rhythm of your pack. If you're following, trust your leader, find his rhythm of consistent forward movement, and stick to it. Find and experience the flow of the road and the road of life.

33 Joining a Group Doesn't Make You Any Less of an Individual

There's a time to blend in, like when you're riding on the highway, but there's also a time to be an individual. Believe it or not, joining a great organization increases your individuality and encourages it. It does not stifle it. When you're part of a group, the right leadership encourages your differences and unique talents and allows you to excel in unpredictable ways.

As members of an organization that rides the same brand of bike, my friends and I sure look, ride, and act differently. True individuals and unusual characters are the core of what makes any organization unique and competitive.

We all conform to some degree. Just as businessmen wear suits and ties, we ride Harleys and wear our colors. So the challenge is to make sure that no two bikes look, feel, or ride the same. Why blend into the crowd when you're in an environment of freedom? Why lose yourself to the masses? A "well-organized group" is composed of many different parts that all have one thing in common, whereas a crowd is composed of many individuals who have very little, if anything, in common.

Very few make it to the top of the heap by remaining ordinary. You not only have the right to be an individual, but, for the good of your organization, you have the obligation to continue to change and get better. So why linger in the background with the majority? We already have enough people riding in the middle of the road. Break away and test the fringes.

A good example of individuality was a member of our group back in the sixties and seventies. He was as rough and tough as the rest of us, a former navy man and a championship wrestler. You could always depend on him, he was always there. His one compulsion was his house—his "castle," he called it. His front yard was a textbook example of anal compulsiveness. Colored rocks were neatly arranged in rows and he worked incessantly to keep it straight and neat. He also didn't allow any drugs of any sort on his premises. He was a real individual who knew what he wanted and maintained his own individuality. And yet, like I said, he was the most loyal club member in the organization.

What about the company you keep or the organization you have built around yourself? Are you distinguishable from the rest yet still considered a "company" man? Do you feel comfortable among the members of your group or are you just faking it?

It's no accident that I ride a loud bike, have fun partying, and proudly wear a colorful patch on my back. Those around me do, too. I've never felt any security in joining the mainstream. I prefer to walk a little out of step. Within my organization, I have expressed my individuality by being myself.

34 Don't Live for a Good Funeral

Why do we wait until exceptional people die before reaching out to honor them? Why do we miss partying with one another while we're all still alive? Or worse, why do we overlook someone we know who happens to feel alone, is down on their luck, or is in need of our help and company as a comrade or friend? In some groups, when a living member reaches a landmark year, their organization honors them by presenting them with plaques, awards, dinners, parties, rides, and most important, they constantly celebrate the brotherhood and the longevity they share now. Today. Ten-year anniversaries of riding with a club are treated as a big deal.

Motorcycle clubs are known for staging elaborate funerals. I don't like funerals because I think they are held too late.

When a bike rider dies, funerals are a loud, massive, and colorful show of respect. Although I respect those who attend funerals for the express purpose of honoring a brother, and while it's an amazing show of solidarity when hundreds, sometimes thousands, of motorcycles converge on a cemetery, I can't help thinking about how all the resources that go into funerals—the flowers, the limos, the coffin, the airfares—how all that expense could easily go toward something else that benefits those left behind to carry on.

Living life is what is important. What goes on your gravestone is something you'll never see. You'll never hear the eulogies or read the obits or talk about yourself after you're gone, so listen carefully now because they are talking about you, believe it or not.

When my doctor told me I had only a few months to live, I didn't brood or sulk or think, *Poor me*. Instead, I started riding faster, harder, and louder. Death sounds like a mighty dull, slow, and dreary process. That's why I hope to put it off for as long as possible. While I accept the constant risk and inevitability of death, as for funerals, I don't like 'em. I'll choose a fast ride with the living over a slow ride with the dead any day.

35 Controlled Anger Is a Powerful Weapon

Anger takes up a lot of time, energy, and resources, and in the long run gets you nowhere until you understand it and then act on it.

Anger, like war, can be approached as a strategic art. By its very nature, anger is a natural human reaction to a situation. But it doesn't have to be acted upon violently. Anyone can get angry. Anger can manifest itself in different ways. Kick the dog. Punch the wall. Yell and scream. Kick ass. Even if you're just letting off steam, there's not much to gain if you let your anger get out of control. Kicking someone's ass—now, that's another story. If you're going to expend your energy through anger or rage, the secret is to get something out of it. Don't expect blind anger to accomplish anything. However, if it's directed and focused, why not use it? To me, the concept of "anger management" is not necessarily about containing your anger, it's about accomplishing something with it and going beyond it.

Here's exactly how I get maximum mileage out of my anger. First, I make sure that I'm angry with the right person, at the right time, for the right reason, with the right intensity, and for the right duration.

Let's go through the steps.

Say I'm angry, but I am at the point where I'm still rational and able to see straight, which means I've gotten over the "blind with rage" part of being angry. I use the old method of counting to ten (slowly) before acting. I make sure I don't misdirect my anger at the wrong person, which is what we irrationally or carelessly tend to do. If I'm angry with Joe but I punch Bob off his bike because he happens to ride by, or because he's smaller than Joe, that doesn't help me accomplish my beef with Joe. Go ahead and get pissed off and act on whoever deserves it.

Acting on your anger is central. Kicking someone's ass days or even months after the fact does little or no good. Think first, then respond immediately. It's a clear reaction to your anger, and you've not only made your point, but there's going to be little confusion as to when and why the other guy on the other side of the table is nursing a swollen jaw.

Getting angry for the right reason has to do with identification. Work on your anger threshold, and go to the mat for only the important reasons as opposed to raising hell for trivial reasons. If someone who borrows my bike accidentally wrecks it, and even if I was dumb enough to lend it to him, my anger might be justifiable.

How long you stay angry tells a lot about your temperament. Know when to let go. Act on your anger, then move on. If you stay angry, or worse, hold grudges for weeks and months, you are harboring and festering and accomplishing nothing. It's an indication of extreme weakness and pettiness when someone stays angry even after everything is settled. If all parties have signed a treaty and you're still stewing, get over it. That is, unless we're talking about revenge, and that's a whole other story.

Don't let your anger stay on the stove like a kettle of boiling water. I find that if I'm angry with my friend or old lady, and I let my anger be known immediately, it gets resolved quickly. If I remain angry with my enemy or my competition, and I keep it inside, I am doing myself and those around me a big disservice.

36 You Win a War by Kicking the Enemy's Ass, Not by Negotiating with Them

Conflict is a clash of thoughts on the same idea between two parties. Simple enough, right? But the end result of conflict is victory, and many times that gets foggy. The biggest reason it does is that we start bartering, negotiating—whatever—and don't get something resolved quickly.

We go to war so that we may live in peace. I see value in war, although it's an expensive proposition and should be your last resort. War requires absolute commitment. Peace won't come until you're entirely prepared to confront your enemy and make sacrifices back home.

In a declaration in the 1960s to Lyndon Johnson, then president of the United States, I offered to go out and fight the war in Vietnam along with quite a few of my friends, as private citizens. Whether or not that war was winnable is still hotly debated. My thought was that we would win some battles, but, more important, we would become a symbol for the rest of the American public to get off their asses and get involved. *Just get the damn war over with*, we thought. As history tells it, we were not granted the right to go over to Vietnam and fight. The war went on and on, lots of money was spent, many people were killed, and if you ask me today what was accomplished, I couldn't begin to tell you.

I am using the example of Vietnam for a reason. The conflict began for a reason, but as the days and months grew into years, that conflict, that major disagreement, grew so intricately muddled that after a while people didn't even know what they were fighting for. At the end, nothing was really resolved. The years of skirmishes and battles did not result in a victory or even a resolution.

I fear the same is now going on in the Mideast. What is the battle plan, what is the war we want to win? The enemy is not defined; he is invisible. It is big government money against goatherders, it seems. But again, innocent people are being killed and the majority of the people in this country only have a vague idea of what is really going on, what the conflict is, and what we are trying to accomplish.

Conflict is a part of everyday life. Accept that and you are ahead of the pack. Identify your conflicts and "kick ass" in any way you see fit, from the easiest method of simply leaving and avoiding it to the most direct method of using your fists. A conflict is resolved only if it is addressed.

37 To Get Wet You Have to Get in the Swimming Pool

Democracy isn't a spectator sport. It is very much a participatory one. To make it work, everyone has to play.

While I tend to resist government intervention by not relying on the government to solve my problems, I strongly believe in the democratic form of government, and I recognize that voting is a fundamental right, privilege, freedom, responsibility, and obligation.

Half of America seems to be sitting on the couch criticizing; the other half seems to run things. Have you taken charge, beginning with your own life? Or are you sitting on the sidelines watching and critiquing less talented people who are running things for you? One of the penalties for refusing to participate in a democracy is being ordered around.

That's why we motorcycle riders are forced to wear helmets. If everyone who rode or owned a motorcycle objected to the government's insistence on helmet wearing, then the helmet law could be done away with. But some riders don't care, are too lazy, are sheep, and go along with everything, so . . . the helmet law exists. This is an example of democracy in action. And dealing with any form of governing body within a democracy works the same way.

This is not a call for you to run for office. Far from it. This is a call to the wild and the young to instigate the next wave of change. Think about how much better life might be if we weren't so content watching mediocre a-holes run our affairs. There are no honest people in the wings waiting to take over from the mediocre and the dishonest. It's down to you, and believe it when I say that one person can make a difference. Whether it's work, play, government, relationships, or family, you've got to jump in, take charge, and accept responsibility. Don't wait for another man to come along and steal your old lady. Don't wait for a government or social-service agency to come along and raise your kid.

Be the best you can be, and then use your talents to have a positive impact on others. Jump in and put experience, good sense, and expertise back to work. Get what you want, make the world a better place for yourself, and then it will be a better place for others, too. Otherwise, we're doomed to continue living in a world where the richest and not necessarily the most honest and selfless rise to the top of the power heap. Do you know somebody with an untapped mountain of potential and strength? If only we could see the same potential in ourselves as others see in us. If only we could swap brains and vantage points and see ourselves through the eyes of those who admire us. We would go through life walking taller, with more confidence in our actions, our ideas, and ourselves.

During the fifties and sixties, America was more of a nation of joiners than it is now. There was an abundance of hot-rod and motorcycle clubs, social clubs, bowling leagues, various kinds of special-interest clubs, lodges, fraternities, sororities, sporting teams, charitable groups, church and religious groups, and business associations; people of all ages joined and belonged to such groups. Now everything is far more specialized and suited only for the individual.

Now we seem to be a country composed of many little societies. Everything comes through the television and the Internet. Everyone has become a vicarious watcher, an ogler. We are amused and captivated by these screen technologies. We order gifts and buy land over them, jerk off in front of them, order plane tickets, play combat games, and here's the important part—we watch the NASCAR races instead of racing on the back streets ourselves. We watch sports rather than participate outdoors. We've evolved into a nation composed primarily of watchers and critics instead of doers and participants. Our heroes have become those who have the courage to do what we're too damned lazy to do ourselves. Americans sit in front of their computers, soaking in porn privately instead of hitting the streets and attracting and interacting with real women. I make it a point to get on my bike at least once a day, fly my colors, ride fast and loud, and show the town and myself that I exist.

If you sit back and watch while others do, especially if you have talents, leadership abilities, answers to questions, or solutions to problems, you're guilty of promoting mediocrity. If, out of laziness and complacency, you'd rather let somebody else "do it," whatever the reason, get up off your ass and get out there. If you're a master mechanic, there's a bike club that could use you. If you're a lawyer, there are organizations that need help getting their people out of trouble. If you have a nose for money, there are lots of people that need to know how to raise funds in order to survive. There's not an organization out there that couldn't use a little more help from talented people.

What angers me is when America sits on its lard ass. What's worse is when we sit on skills that could be put to use for the greater good.

If you don't like what the people in charge are doing to your neighborhood, city, town, or state, you have the right to vote them out. If you think the guy in the White House makes Americans look like mugs to the rest of the world, then vote him out. If you don't want your kids to inherit the leaders we have, then vote them out. If you're sick of the two-party system, then vote for a third party.

Get in the pool and get wet and splash around and make a difference because if you don't, then you're just another critic, another complainer, who is bringing nothing to the table but a plate of excuses.

38 Don't Trade Freedom for the New Security

What patriot needs a PATRIOT Act?

Be that person who stands up not only for your immediate family circle, your old lady, your brother, your coworker, and your friends, but also for the neighbor down the street you hardly know. There's a quote written by a minister, Martin Niemoller, in Germany, in 1933: "First they came for the Jews . . . and I didn't speak up because I was not a Jew . . . then they came for me and by that time there was no one left to speak up for me."

I've lived (by choice) in the crosshairs of my adversaries and my country. While for years I've enjoyed the support of a brotherhood, I've seen a lot of people look the other way when the cops were breaking down my door. We may think we live in the freest nation in the world, but that doesn't mean you can relax for even a second. The day after they come for me, they might be coming for you next. Sound paranoid? Not so fast.

Over the past few years, since 9/11, we've seen our federal government grab more power with the passage of the PATRIOT Act. Since 2001, it's much easier for our government to define an unrecognized group's activity as terrorism, targeting not only scary people on motorcycles, but also various religious and ethnic groups. The potential danger to our liberty and freedom is now twofold. First, if you're seen as a "subversive," and second, if certain of your acts are perceived as "subversive activity," you can now be prosecuted for committing terrorist acts. The government today is operating with unprecedented power and leeway. Look out for your constitutional rights to free association, speech, and travel. The rules have been amended a bit since 9/11.

Government intervention spills over into our daily lives, at home, on the job, and on the road. In doing everything from putting money in the bank and obtaining a driver's license to the simple process of boarding an airplane, we are now subject to a whole new set of rules and regulations since the passage of the PATRIOT Act. They say it is for our protection, but it is simply not being done right. In short, a lot of the new screening and protection methods are being carried out in a humiliating fashion and by robots in rote step-by-step methods that insult the average American.

In theory, when a government increases its power during times of emergency and war, such an extension of power is intended to be temporary. Most governments somehow fail or forget to give power back to the people once the peace is restored. Too many Americans seem resigned to hand over their rights in the name of security and this endless war on terrorism. Unfortunately, the PATRIOT Act doesn't make me feel safer or more secure. It disturbs my libertarian heart much more than it comforts it. As Ben Franklin once warned us, when we hand over freedom for security, we deserve neither freedom nor security.

The best way to protect freedom for ourselves is to protect freedom for everybody.

39 The Bigger the Group, the Smaller the Ideal

The world we live in, our society, our culture is a product of what we all have made it. The oversize government and all of the organizations have been created because of our failure as individuals to stand up for ourselves. Today, these overruling powers tell us what *we* really want, how *we* should be living, and almost how *we* should conduct ourselves every day.

On the street level, I think that we can all get along if we want to. It will take a lot of individual effort and respect. We'd have to learn to leave one another alone. People can interact to bring about changes and accomplish things without having someone overseeing everything. But a lot of people don't see it that way and this brings into play forces to look over us—bigger companies, bigger government, more policemen, more enlisted men, armies, more people in uniforms. Every day the other side gets bigger.

Some years back, a bunch of bike clubs proposed to sit down together and talk about becoming a more

united front against our common enemies, forming a co-
alition of sorts. In other words, one big giant bike-rider
conglomerate.

I was against it for many reasons. What was being
proposed was a situation that I considered unthinkable.
We were going to fight fire with fire and what was the
point? We get bigger and bigger, but what happens to
the individual and what he wants? Where does the "I" fit
into such a large group?

These were just some of the questions I brought up
and that led me to believe that fusing a bunch of bike
clubs together was not the best idea to cross the table. I
wanted to belong to a group that I could put my arms
around, a group where I knew everybody and their characteristics rather than a lot of stats and numbers. I didn't
want to belong to another army. I wanted to still see and
be myself, do what I wanted to do, and not be influenced
by a group that didn't even know my name.

40 Give Your People the Freedom to Screw Up

Everyone should have the freedom to screw up.

We learn from our mistakes, pure and simple. Most of us can only improve after we know what it feels like to have screwed up.

Running an organization with an iron fist and by instilling the fear of failure just doesn't work. To be productive and creative, your people need room to move, air to breathe, space to expand, and, most important, the opportunity and luxury to plain mess up once in a while. If you run your ship in a climate of fear, it breeds distrust, backstabbing, disharmony, and, worse, mutiny. The overthrow comes when someone else who wants to step up and run the show comes up with a better definition of fear.

While I was an officer in one of the most renowned bike organizations in the world, I, of course, got challenged for that position many times. I came to expect it and it kind of kept things going. I never backed down and never lost the position until I resigned. But that didn't mean I didn't have to keep my guard up at all times. There was always someone, be it a cop or a biker from another club, who wanted to go from a zero to a hero by trying to knock me off. No one ever did because I never let them.

The positive effects of good and strong leadership last well beyond the influence of one person's ego or even the life of a single organization. Being in an organization where, if you screw up, you are hung out to dry and ridiculed just doesn't work. Where there is respect and action, and the freedom to mess up once in a while, you'll find that your organization's performance will not only get better, but its batting average between doing the right thing and screwing up will improve.

A failure is really a breakdown in operation. Two points don't meet, two pieces don't fit, and it is the wise leader who sees and understands that everything can be repaired to some degree, even if it ends up different from the way it was originally formulated. From failure comes one of two things: further failure or repair. I try to inspire those around me to go for the repair method. There's no future in failure.

An exemplary leader inspires those around him to want to excel, exceed themselves, and do their best. That starts with a leader who trusts himself and his organization enough to accept failure and go beyond it.

41 When You Got Nothing to Prove, Just Put It on Cruise Control

Whenever I'm on a long haul on the inter-state, I notice something different about Corvettes. Corvettes have always been one of my fa-vorite cars, and years ago, I collected them. I entered the cooler ones in car shows and won a few trophies. I even got busted once, thanks to one of my Corvettes.

I had just entered my 'Vette in a car show in Oak-land. She took second prize. The next day, they ran a pic-ture of the car and me in the newspaper. All my friends saw it. Unfortunately, so did an auditor working for the IRS. After seeing the picture of the car in the paper, he looked up my tax return. Because of my reported in-come (low) and the value of the car (high), I got nailed.

Corvettes have power. I consider them one of the original American muscle cars. These days, they can carry up to 350 or 405 horsepower with a 5.7-liter V-8 en-gine, a six-speed manual transmission, and titanium ex-haust components. With power to spare, these babies can reach speeds of over 170 miles per hour, though

I rarely see them do it. Today, most of the Corvettes I pass on the highway cruise the slow lane, purring along, with absolutely nothing to prove.

In my book, that's the way to be. Like a Corvette. Powerful. Fast. Smart. Beautiful. With absolutely nothing to prove. That's why you often see Corvettes rumbling slowly down the highway—that is, until it's time to put the hammer down, step on the gas, and blow everybody away.

There's something to be said for having strength and power but not using it. Having strength and power while others know you have it, but still not using it. Saving it for the times that matter. I like the idea of keeping power in reserve until it's time to use it. Part of the privilege of power is traveling at your own chosen pace.

42 Trust Your Gut. It Doesn't Need Any Oil or Batteries.

I do a lot of signings at Harley dealerships. They used to be the places where guys who worked on their bikes went when they got stuck, needed some advice, or needed a part. Today, Harley shops are dealerships and department stores combined, with as much of the store devoted to leatherwear, wallets, jewelry, sunglasses, and clothing as for motorcycles and service bays.

Recently, I noticed a display on the countertop, a fancy chromed oil temperature gauge. A couple of the guys stood around looking at it and chuckling. I learned it ran about three hundred dollars.

"Not on my bike," said one rider, laughing.

"Me neither," said another. "I don't need a damned chrome gauge. I can tell the oil temperature by touching the oil tank with my thumb."

Of course my friend was joking. I don't recommend taking your bike's temperature by touching the tank. What he wasn't joking about was not spending three hundred bucks for a dipstick with a thermometer. Instead of ponying up three bills for a chromed goodie, guys like him would much rather rely on their instincts and their "feel" for their machines. Riding along the road, you can reach down and feel the heat right below you while still looking ahead, as you ought to.

That got me to thinking. Which is the more sophisticated device, the gauge or the thumb? I'd say the thumb—by far. The thumb is what separates us humans from machines. The body is a miraculous piece of equipment connected to a mechanism far more advanced than the biggest, most expensive supercomputer ever built. I'm talking about the human brain. We're lord and master over one of the most miraculous machines, our bodies.

What attracted me to riding motorcycles in the first place was that nothing else so seamlessly combines machinery with the human body than riding a motorcycle. Every so often I need to remind myself about how the synergy of the brain and the body relates to the mechanical world. William Burroughs referred to the body as a "soft machine." It's the highest piece of technology we've got. Take care of it, and use it, and most of all listen to it.

43 Discover Your Limits by Exceeding Them

How much is enough and what happens when you've had more than enough?

One of the first day jobs I had after I dropped out of high school was working at the Granny Goose potato-chip factory. My sister got me the gig. Outside of the chance to meet a few of the factory girls, the job was mostly a drag. I'd ride my motorcycle to work. All night long we'd fill giant cylinder containers with potato chips and stack them high. But I did learn one important lesson.

I happened to love potato chips, and Granny Goose makes the best. You haven't lived until you've had a hot, fresh potato chip just out of the fryer, before they've been sorted, salted, and seasoned. I could have eaten a ton of them.

One day I tried to.

You've heard the saying "Too much of a good thing . . ." Well, double that. Apparently, the guys I worked with had shared the same experience. As they watched me indulge to excess, they already knew what was going to happen. It was something I would have to learn on my own. By the end of my shift, I'd eaten so many potato chips I was ready to puke. Nobody warned me. I think that was the whole point of the lesson. You have to learn about your own excesses by yourself. We all have different ones—be it food, alcohol, drugs, gambling . . . hell, the list could go on and on.

I would go on to have the same experience with other excesses like cocaine and cigarettes. Eventually, I figured it out. When you love something so much, and you have a seemingly endless supply, and there's nobody willing to jump in and save you from yourself, in the long run you're being dealt a favor. Sometimes we need to go completely over the top to find out exactly what constitutes enough, or for that matter, too much.

I don't use cocaine now, I don't smoke Camel cigarettes anymore, and I don't eat too many Granny Goose potato chips. I've had my fill. I experienced my limits, and as a result, I no longer have the slightest desire to overindulge in those areas. I learned something valuable that nobody could have taught or explained to me in a million years. By finding out on my own what constitutes too much of a good thing, I eliminated the temptation and the attraction of excess forever. I now know the meaning of the word *enough,* and I stick to it.

44 Quitting Time Is Not the End. It Is the Beginning.

Sometimes it's not a good idea to persist.
Sometimes it's better to quit while you've got the legs to walk away, quit while you're ahead, as they say.

While I'm well known for riding a Harley, I've got nothing against cars and trucks. I'm just a far better rider than I am a driver. All my life, I've managed to dodge even the craziest drivers on my bike. Riding comes natural, but driving to me is a chore.

I remember talking to an older bike-rider friend of mine, a woman. She dramatically informed me that she was selling her Harley. She'd recently had a couple of close calls on the highway on her bike, experiences that spooked her, robbing her of her confidence and poise. Even so, I think she was looking for me to try to talk her out of selling the bike. But I wouldn't.

Doing what you love includes staying on top of your physical game and knowing when to walk away. As we get older, reflexes slip by a fraction of a second. Unfortunately, a fraction of a second is all it takes to end up spread-eagled across the highway, collecting gravel and road rash. In the past, I've seen quite a few bike crashes. Many of those accidents resulted from momentary lapses of concentration or ability.

I could have told my friend to tough it out, to hang in there and keep riding, but that's what she expected to hear from me. But as a friend, I put it to her straight. Clearly, her confidence was damaged beyond repair. She was now a danger on the road, to herself and to others. The highway was trying to tell her something. She needed to listen. She didn't need me handing out bad advice.

My response took her by surprise. Then I gave her some names of a couple of ladies I knew who were looking to buy a nice bike for cheap.

A while later I ran into her at the auto parts store. She was buying truck parts. She'd sold the bike and now she was driving a small Ford pickup. She was holding her small granddaughter by the hand.

"Sonny, you were right. I'm glad I sold the bike. I miss it sometimes, but now I have other obligations."

My friend had accomplished something important. She figured out the best time to throw in her hand and fold.

45 Individuality Is the Most Precious Freedom

Do you believe that an almighty federal government poses a potential threat today to the basic rights and liberty of ordinary citizens?

If you do, you're not alone.

Every man and woman has the right to live their lives their way so long as they don't interfere with the equal rights or safety of others. Property rights and the right of self-ownership (which means, literally, owning yourself) are the core of my beliefs, and if I'm reading the Constitution of the United States right, they are the basic principles of being an American.

As an American, I do have the "right" to pursue an education, own a house, apply for a government subsidy, or seek protections installed by the government for my businesses, but I don't choose to use these services afforded me because I value doing those things myself.

When I hear the word *rights,* I think in terms of an individual's right to pursue his own life and liberty and to own property. Not the "rights" that I am due from the government.

What worries me most about America now is how our government fights crime. I see detecting and prosecuting crime as primarily a local function, not a national one. While I may not like the police force, and I don't, I understand that each community maintains a police force as part of a program to provide basic city services (even if I choose not to use them). A national police force treats me and my problems like a case number. Individuality is gone.

The concept of law enforcement has taken an evil turn over the past few years, since 9/11. Even before 9/11, law enforcement had strayed from being a city- and state-run function to an enormous federal endeavor. Before the era of homeland security, ask yourself, How effective was the FBI and the CIA in working together? There are now over fifty-two federal government agencies whose employees have the power to carry a firearm and arrest people.

Freedom and liberty, as we interpret them in America, are young concepts in historical terms, under three hundred years old. What bothers a lot of people, especially those in the Middle East who hate Americans, is that we Americans seem fixated on individual rights and liberty. Yet I find our freedom relative. By relative, I mean, it all comes down to how much or how little the government has on you. It is possible to live outside the law, but once "they" have you on their radar screen and you require their subsidies in order to survive, you're a marked man.

One of our most basic constitutional rights is the freedom of association and assembly. One way a bureaucratic government agency can gain more control over an individual is to limit who they associate with. For example, the first thing a parole officer or a judge might slap on someone like me is a nonassociation clause, which specifically states, as a condition of my release on parole, who I can and cannot associate with. Granted, parole, from the standpoint of personal freedom, is like still being in prison. Yet I've had judges tell me that they would release me if I promised not to associate with my friends who ride motorcycles. I told them where to stick it. I'd rather remain locked down in jail than live under such a restriction. Who you associate with is a very powerful aspect of your life, and don't think the powers that be don't know that.

Too many laws are passed every day. It's all these new rules, regulations, and the bureaucracy that are bogging us down, whether you're riding a motorcycle, hiring someone at your company, or adding a room to your house.

Back to the basics. And the utmost, the bottom tier, the foundation of the American Constitution, is freedom for the individual and his right to exercise it in any manner or form that he pleases so long as he doesn't infringe on the rights of others.

46 My Body Is My Business

What do motorcycle helmets have to do with freedom?

I can't think of a better way to exhibit the relationship between my personal liberty and government intervention than by bringing up the issues surrounding the motorcycle helmet laws in America. It's a fight that riders have been involved in for many years. And we've fought it alone. The motorcycle companies have been conspicuously absent. Once, when I was testifying in front of a committee of the California state legislature, one assemblyman threatened to introduce a bill stipulating that "only Sonny Barger be required to wear a helmet."

I'm hard-pressed to find a more freedom-loving bunch of people than motorcycle riders. Motorcyclists in general are a segment of American society that is not fond of big government, especially when the government dictates what we must wear on our noggins while riding. It's hard to find any wisdom behind any government agency picking a fight with motorcycle riders. We stand up and fight for what we believe in. We attract attention. We've spent years lobbying, demonstrating, and opposing legislatures across the country who try to pass laws that have to do not only with helmets, but with how we choose to modify our motorcycles.

You're probably thinking, *What's the problem with wearing a helmet? Just behave, wear one, and shut up.* My main point of philosophical opposition is the principle of personal freedom of choice, and simply put, I don't like being told what and what not to wear while riding. Riders hate helmets for a variety of practical reasons: reduced peripheral vision and hearing, increased wind shear and weight, heat buildup, and uncomfortable chin straps.

In our attempts to fight helmet legislation, we've endured just about every trick that arrogant big government and special interests could pull. The cards have been stacked against us right from the start. Universal mandatory helmet laws were favored by the big insurance companies, who were better served by reducing the number of motorcycle riders on the road. In every state that has adopted a helmet law, ridership dropped from ten to twenty percent. It was easier to reduce the pool of motorcyclist targets than to educate drivers on how to avoid hitting us. And since the medical profession owes its livelihood to the insurance companies, it seems to me that the doctors turned out to assert falsely that helmets effectively reduced accident injuries.

During the early 1990s, the feds blackmailed those states not enacting mandatory helmet laws by limiting their share of federal highway funding. Fortunately, a Harley-riding senator, Ben Nighthorse Campbell, rode to the rescue and helped to repeal that foolishness before California knuckled under.

The overall picture is pretty confusing and discouraging. Out of fifty states, only four—Colorado, Illinois, Iowa, and New Hampshire—are one hundred percent helmet-law-free. Of the remaining forty-six states, nineteen have full helmet laws, requiring that all motorcycle riders wear helmets. Twenty states have helmet laws that exempt adult riders eighteen years or older. An additional seven states require riders between the ages of eighteen and twenty to wear a helmet.

Sound perplexing? We haven't even talked about what constitutes "approved headgear" and "safety helmets" and in which state. Every time you ride cross-country, unless you're an expert on helmet laws, you may find yourself pulled over for noncompliance. Because of differing state regulations, technically, riders could be required to pack different varieties of helmets in order to comply with each state's different helmet law.

It all adds up to one government-meddling mess.

So what does this have to do with freedom for Americans who don't ride motorcycles? Besides the waste of taxpayer dollars instituting and enforcing these laws, the bottom line is this: you've got a segment of society willing to accept responsibility for its own actions and safety. Nobody's more aware of the safety factors and the dangers involving motorcycle riding than motorcycle riders themselves. Yet why do big government and special interests persist in forcing their wills and agendas onto a slice of the population who are so notoriously freedom loving?

The irony is that I choose to wear a full-faced helmet. I often wear one (though not all the time) in order to control the dust and airflow, since, after having throat-cancer surgery, I breathe through my neck. I consider a helmet to be a necessary riding accessory. A lot of us do. No cop had to tell me. No politician had to pass a law forcing me. I figured it out for myself.

The debate over helmet laws is a classic American struggle over individual freedom and self-determination. I believe in a rider's right to choose. How free are we, really, if government and corporate special interests insist on usurping the responsibilities that we already accept in the first place? Maybe you don't ride a motorcycle. Wherever your interests lie, and whatever you choose to do for a living or for pleasure, I hope there's no government or law enforcement agency looking over your shoulder, telling you how and how not to enjoy yourself or further your enterprise.

When I think further about the helmet laws as a very good example of big-government intervention, many other things about our bodies come to mind—like suicide. If I choose to take my own life, why should the government have the right to intervene? This is wholly an individual's decision: no one else can make it for him. And yet there is the government stepping in and making what should be a simple sacred act something that is unlawful. And it is only here in America, the land of the free. Once again, death is big business here. There is a statistic that is staggering: over seventy percent of the medical bills you have your entire life are spent during the last two months of your life. And guess where all that money is pouring? Into those cute little pharmaceutical conglomerates.

If I want to live in a high-risk or dangerous situation, I don't want the government telling me, first, that

I can't and, second, that if I choose to, then what I should or should not be wearing. It is up to the individual to determine all of that. Anything that affects me and my well-being should not be something that is imposed on me by my government.

47

You Gotta Learn to Listen, You Gotta Listen to Learn

Are you listening or just waiting to talk?

One of the by-products of losing my vocal cords is that I had to reinvent the way I communicated. Most of us just open our mouths and talk away. But after my surgery, I had to learn to vibrate the muscles in my throat in a special way before I talked. Talking now requires the use of one hand, one thumb, trapping air over a plastic valve placed in my throat, so that I'm able to vibrate a muscle that forms words. It took a lot of time and work to get the hang of it. Now it's a natural process, a more exacting process that ultimately enhanced my communication skills. But who would have thought? Not me.

One of the side effects (and benefits) of relearning to talk was relearning the whole process of communication. My method of talking now requires a whole extra step, but it has given me another dimension to the act of communication, and that is listening. Now, when somebody's talking to me, I not only hear the words, but

I study faces, mannerisms, and since I intentionally hesitate a few moments before answering, I find that I'm able to think a little more about what's behind the words people say. My level of comprehension has increased. I've become a more succinct communicator. I say what I mean, I mean what I say, and I don't run off at the mouth.

The next time you're in a discussion with someone, before automatically responding, stop for a moment. Slow down the process and force yourself to think before speaking. Mentally compose what you want to say, and then express it carefully. Don't answer so darned fast. Don't interrupt, and try not to talk over anyone (though sometimes there's no alternative). Become a true listener, both to the words being spoken to you and to what's behind the words of the person communicating with you.

Devote your full attention to the person you're talking to. Don't slight them by being distracted by other people in the room. Make them feel special by looking them straight in the eye.

If I regained my former voice tomorrow, I know that the qualities of being a good listener would stay with me. I would still look people in the eye, give them my full attention, and reap the benefits of winning the fundamental respect of the person I'm communicating with. I hope you don't have to lose your vocal cords in order to become a better communicator and listener. All you have to do is remember to stop, look, and listen. Think and then respond.

48 Sitting on the Fence Is for the Birds

I started challenging the corporate slave state early on in life.

School and I didn't fit well together; there were far too many rules and things we had to do and it seemed to me that all we did was sit there. I wanted to be outside doing something.

I've always been someone that wants to be doing something. Not talking about it or thinking about what could be done, but doing it. I have always felt my first impulse or instinct was right and I've gotten this far, so something must have been working.

But as I have gone through life, I have seen too many people sitting on the sidelines watching and I think it must be one of two things that makes them do that: fear or laziness.

Fear could take the form of being afraid they might be wrong or, even more, fearful for their lives, reputations, and well-being.

Laziness is another thing altogether. That's a habit

developed by people who just float through life and let others do things for them and are not interested in making a difference anyway.

In the late sixties, there were a lot of antiwar demonstrations going on and in particular a lot going on in the Bay Area, where I lived. I knew my position on the war, and rather than not getting involved, I did. With seven or eight of my fellow club members, I went to a demonstration just to see what was going on. The club was basically apolitical, but some of us were veterans and had served and we didn't like the way the demonstrators were treating the Vietnam veterans. They were not only blaming them but ridiculing them.

So we went out to a major demonstration to make our point just like the demonstrators against the war were making theirs. Fair is fair. We wanted to make it clear where we stood on the war as well, and guess what, we were for it.

Big surprise to everybody.

I felt like the peaceniks were only agitating and calling names and really didn't have specific complaints except for the fact that they wanted the war to stop. They weren't getting anything done really, except for looking like heroes in one another's eyes.

We made our point and left.

If something is wrong, as I have said before, it is up to you to fix it. Don't just sit there, do something rather than obeying and criticizing. Challenge the systems of control. Only you can change your world.

49 Blood Makes Everything Slippery

I took my inspiration from a movie; you can take yours from wherever you want.

Johnny or Chino? Who's the man?

Over fifty years after its debut, *The Wild One* remains an important movie to me. It's a movie about freedom on a motorcycle that sparked a revolution among teenagers of the fifties and on into the sixties. It was my first realization of freedom.

Most of the film's fans identify with Marlon Brando's character, Johnny Strabler. Brando, who did a lot of his own riding in the film, influenced a later crop of rebel movies and actors, including *Rebel Without a Cause, Jailhouse Rock,* and much later, *Easy Rider*. Aside from being banned in England for fourteen years and selling a lot of black leather jackets and motorcycles, *The Wild One* did only respectable business. But it set off a whole new genre of film, the low-budget bike picture (including *Hell's Angels '69* and *Hell's Angels on Wheels,* in which I participated). Some maintain that *The Wild One* set motorcycling back years, but for me, it pushed it into a proper perspective.

The Wild One was the first movie I saw that put the feel of motorcycle riding in a realistic light. It depicted motorcycles ridden in tight military squadron formation, the principle from which many an early motorcycle club was born. In the movie, there are drag races in the street. Doughnuts are spun in the dust. Women are chased and ogled at.

The Wild One woke up American youth during the sleepy conforming Eisenhower fifties. It sparked a rebellion, causing kids like me to question their own views on authority and freedom. *The Wild One* hit a nerve and jump-started the cultural revolution of the sixties. All sparked by motorcycle riders.

During the final scene of the movie, Johnny smiles. But Chino, the Lee Marvin character, doesn't stop grinning throughout the entire film, even when he's knocked silly off his bike. While everyone else deals with the calamity and confusion, and while Johnny is nearly broken by the system, Chino is the only guy who truly has life by the balls. He is the hero who is free and rides, off camera, into the sunset.

Most people are raised to be quiet, to conform, to obey. They're told they should go through life avoiding risks or fights or trouble or whatever. We're raised to think that blood, violence, and sex are things to be avoided. But watching Chino made me realize that it's not that simple. For some of us, living outside of the rules, outside the norm, outside of where things are safe and predictable and boring, is where life is at its best.

Blood makes everything slippery.

50 Keep Things Fresh by Replacing the Tires and Checking the Oil

How big is your world, and is it getting bigger or smaller?

The size of your world is in direct proportion to how much courage you have to fill it, change it, and even leave it. During my last days in Oakland, I felt that my way of life was shrinking. As traffic clogged the roadways (and age clogged my arteries), even the sky seemed to be closing in on me. I had a couple of heart attacks. California, the original motorcyclists' paradise, seemed fenced in and I was shrinking with it. The streets seemed filled with cops. The population numbers told me everything I needed to know. Twenty-seven million people now lived in California. Arizona had six million.

It was time to move on. I was gone.

Those of you who live in places like Montana or the Dakotas know all about space. You understand the concept of open skies. I found out that environment reflects your mood, and my mood was changing for the worse. I was running out of sky, and I felt the need to feel more space. Sonny's rule of thumb: the bigger the sky, the bigger your world, the more room you have to move.

I had experienced the desert near Phoenix while I was in the federal prison there, and became fond of the hot dry climate that seemed to favor my respiratory system. It's also a great place to ride, if you can get away from the city.

My world grew suddenly and dramatically when I moved to the Southwestern United States. It took a bit of courage, first to admit to myself that I needed a change in scenery after many decades, and then to actually move on. Sell the house. Pack up the stuff I'd accumulated over a half century. Leave most of my best friends miles behind. Ride away from my birthplace. But in the end, it was all worth the effort.

The minute I made the commitment to relocate to a place with more room to ride, more sky to look up at, and more air to breathe, I instantly felt my lungs and my world expanding. I could now physically breathe deeper. I felt stronger. Once a free mind is rocked by a new idea and a new environment, it is never the same. Change was great. Once again, I was ridin' high and livin' free. I wasn't sticking around someplace for the sake of sticking around, and that included my home and my relationships.

Fewer laws contribute to living a larger "Barger" life. As California became more and more legislated, I longed for a new Wild Western home front. I'd lived in California since the day I was born. California was no longer the secret paradise. The word was out. Even the gold country seemed crowded. I needed broader horizons, where I could open up the throttle and really let my bike and my life kick loose. For me, that place turned out to be Arizona.

I can already see houses and shops creeping in where there was once dry empty land. I guess it's inevitable. Like the lonesome fugitive my buddy Merle Haggard sings about, I'll be on the run again soon, chased farther and farther up a country road, farther away from the crowds and the housing developments that keep popping up everywhere. It's a fact of life that if you're not running from the law, you only have to stay one step ahead of everyone else, and you'll be okay. I know that now, know that I must keep riding and keep moving.

And I will.

Be free.